# Left of the Loop

12/1/01

Emily:

Dissipation adds life to your years while it subtracts years from your life.

— Tim Br

# Left of the Loop

## A Novel

Tim W. Brown

| Library of Congress Number: | | 2001117687 |
|---|---|---|
| ISBN #: | Softcover | 1-4010-2033-X |





Cover image by Michele Mach.
Author photo by George Burns.

This book was printed in the United States of America.

**To order additional copies of this book, contact:**
Xlibris Corporation
1-888-7-XLIBRIS
www.Xlibris.com
Orders@Xlibris.com

# Contents

THIS BOOK IS DEDICATED TO MARK D. HEDL.

# Acknowledgments

Portions of this book have appeared in *Storyhead, Lumpen, The Fiction Review, Planet Roc, The Squealer, WISdom, American Goat* and *Poked With Sticks*.

This project is partially supported by a grant from the Illinois Arts Council, a state agency, and a Community Arts Assistance Program grant from the City of Chicago Department of Cultural Affairs.

# 1 Spungkdt Arrives

> Poetry has been attacked by an ignorant and frightened bunch of bores who don't understand how it's made, and the trouble with these creeps is they wouldn't know poetry if it came up and buggered them in broad daylight.
>
> —Allen Ginsberg

I was a grad school washout. Finding a year out west falling short of my expectations of the Promised Land, I decided to forsake my plans of earning a master's degree in creative writing and return to Chicago, where, like many thousands before me, I would seek my fortune. My decision came one day in the recognition that I suffered from chronic abdominal upset and that this condition stemmed directly from the academic environment. Each and every day I was in graduate school it felt as though little tractors were bulldozing back in forth in my bowels; on account of several bad experiences, I discovered that students and faculty at the university I attended were the ones piloting those little tractors. Two experiences in particular stood out.

In the fall of that year, I was enrolled in a poetry-writing workshop. One day a student in the class presented a poem, which we all had in our laps on photocopies he passed out the week before. The Semicircle, as I called it, a group of us poets from the English Department and a few townies, too, sat in chairs arranged in a semicircle inside a windowless classroom. Right down the line everyone nodded his or her assent: it was a pretty decent poem. Democracy always was ought after in these workshops, especially when after the votes were cast the results were unanimous: the poem was either a Winner or a Loser. This one was clearly a Winner.

I didn't like it that much, though; it contained lots of drooling description of the poet's motorcycle, stuff like "1000 cc's of hate/ roaring at you," the "you" not exactly spelled out. The poem also described a lot of adolescent police dodging on this motorcycle, so maybe "you" meant the pigs or the fuzz. At any rate, I didn't have anything good to say about the poem, but I didn't want to say anything brutal, unlike the others in this workshop, who would ride your back like mountain lions if you slipped at all away from their conception of poetry, the iambic column, three to five iambs per line. I couldn't not just say anything either, because I drank with this guy a few times and considered him a decent sort, which obligated me to comment on the poem.

So when they got to me I simply said, "I like the way the poem is shaped like the state of Alabama." In fact, it really did resemble maps I had seen of Alabama—the poem was a bit narrower toward the top, gradually widened toward the bottom, then had a one word last line hanging below, sort of like Mobile jutting into the Gulf of Mexico.

The teacher of the workshop looked over his reading glasses as if I just had said the craziest thing he ever heard, and he, I'm sure, had heard plenty of crazy things in his twenty-year career. Then he said something about how thought should go into laying out the poem on the page, and he quickly introduced the next poem we were to critique. He did not explain why the poem was shaped like the state of Alabama, nor did he discern any correlation between the poem's shape and its subject matter. Furthermore, he didn't appear at all to see the resemblance that I saw.

A week or two after this happened I sat in my office at Jackdaw Hall, taking to heart my teacher's words concerning the Alabama poem: "Every poem surely does rely on the way it's composed—the length of lines, even punctuation add to its feel. However, we shouldn't, as it were, miss the trees while staring too much at the forest." Then a poem came to me like most poems I wrote: it just rose up from my lap. I ended up writing a poem about Jackson Pollock, which I laid out across the page in the all-over, random-looking, scattered style of a Pollock painting. When I banged it out on a typewriter, I thought it looked pretty good.

I pulled the sheet out of the typewriter and tacked it to my bulletin board. I raised my coffee cup and drank to it, but after my swallow had gone halfway down, I choked and said, "I'm rebelling against the iambic column. I'm gonna get reamed."

With nothing better in hand, I presented this poem to the next meeting of the workshop, this particular occasion a special one, because the school flew in this famous, eighty-year-old, Pulitzer Prize-winning poet, whom the writing community considered the "Grand Old Man" of American poetry. He gave a terrific reading earlier, but in class he tired easily and turned cranky. He had no patience for my poem, which he dismissed as "an experiment," and neither did the rest of the workshop, who had just drawn blood from a previous poet presenting his work and now smelled blood with mine. As you would expect, a feeding frenzy ensued. One guy went so far as to call my poem "pseudo psychedelic psychobabble." I still can show you tooth marks on my arm from that experience.

After a forty-seven-hour bus ride, spent smoking furiously in the last row, I was welcomed back to Chicago by Stark, my old college roommate and friend for life, at the Greyhound bus station on the corner of Clark and Lake. In order to head out to Stark's loft in the West Loop, we had to ride a Lake Street elevated train to the Halsted stop. "Isn't it weird how 'Clark and Lake' sounds better than 'Lake and Clark?'" he asked. I didn't answer; I just thought to myself that the way the train we rode weaved and bounced twenty feet off the ground thrilled me more than any ride at Disneyland.

"Cool place," I said, after we had descended the stairs from the L platform and began the three-block walk to his loft. Every which way I turned I saw boarded-up storefronts, splintered pallets, crumpled plastic pop bottles, crushed paper cups, mounds of rotting tomatoes and lettuce, windblown newspaper pages, waterlogged cardboard cartons full of tin cans or watermelon rinds, and the ever-present broken liquor bottles and crumbs of shattered windshield glass.

A train roared overhead as we walked. "Watch your back," Stark said. "People can sneak up behind you with all the noise, and there's nobody around to witness it."

This was true; we were the only two humans on the street. "It's, uh, pretty deserted here," I said.

"Things are safe—I was only kidding you. When all the meatpackers leave at three o'clock, it turns into *my* neighborhood."

"I guess you're right," I said, somewhat relieved, but nevertheless watching my back until we had the street door to Stark's building locked behind us.

Later on, as a West Loop veteran, a question I frequently faced from outsiders was this: "Aren't you paranoid somebody will bash in your head with a brick and steal your money when you walk home from the L late at night?"

"Not ever," I would answer. You see, Stark and I understood that nobody with money (except lonely men in search of hookers) was around on the streets surrounding Sangamon, so there were no pickings for potential assailants. In fact, I think the chances of getting mugged or having your purse snatched or shopping bags stolen were a lot higher on the Gold Coast, a neighborhood which by its name practically advertised, "Wanted: Criminals."

Besides, at six-foot-two I'm pretty tall, and I think this fact intimidates, though I'm pretty skinny and have never been especially strong. Stark is closer to average height, but being a drummer, he's built pretty well in his upper body and arms. He also has this untrimmed, evergreen bush hair that gives him the look of a genuine madman. So it was our physical attributes, coupled with the pair of us grumping and growling down the streets and alleys, which scared away anyone who meant us harm. Or at least I liked to think that way.

"This is it," Stark said, pointing to a large steel door on the second floor of 210 North Sangamon. He unlocked a pad lock, threw down a latch and then rolled the door to the side. The door was on tracks and was connected to a whole mess of pulleys and counterweights, reminding me of the door to a boxcar.

"The gate to Fort Sangamon," Stark said, attesting to the mass of what we came to call the big metal sliding steel door.

"No need to worry about anybody breaking in here," I said.

"Nope. The loft's impregnable. I look out my windows like I was up on ramparts."

## *The Ceiling*

When I walked into the loft, my eyes were drawn to the ceiling first. The beams ran north and south; they were wood and painted white. They looked feathered to me, not because I'm near-sighted (even though I am); rather, after decades of neglect the paint was flaking off. Indeed, at the very moment I noticed this, an elevated train rumbled by a half-block away, which caused the floor to vibrate stronger and then weaker, whereupon an off-white powder gradually appeared on my left shoulder.

Intersecting these beams at nearly right angles, there were pipes of various diameters, from thin electrical conduit on up to six-inch piping wrapped in insulation crumbling off like gauze off mummies at the Field Museum.

"I hope the water and the electric don't ever feed into the same line anywhere, especially when I'm in the tub," I said, directing Stark's attention upwards.

"It hasn't happened yet. Just to play it safe, I clamp the lights onto pipes that don't lead anywhere. I figure they're dead." The lights Stark used to illuminate the loft were those coathangery, clothespin things that take a regular hundred-watt bulb. As I looked around, I saw a few were shielded; most, however, were just the bare, harsh, but always crisp, bulb.

Not being totally alien to the luxuries of middle class homes (we both grew up in such places), Stark had a more decorative light of shiny-white spherical steel hanging directly over his desk. One night when he was bored he wrote with an indelible marker the words "Transgrender 64" on this lamp. In all the time I lived left of the Loop, he never explained to me what the phrase meant, but I somehow always found it comforting, like an inspirational phrase tacked to a bulletin board.

One interesting thing Stark had hanging from the ceiling was a chin-up bar he strung up over a vacant twelve-by-twelve-foot stretch of floor in the middle of the loft that he introduced as the "Sangamon Gym." "It's where I do my calisthenics and work out with my dumbbells," he explained. "*When* I work out, I mean. I haven't really done anything there since about two weeks ago when I coughed up a bunch of old boots and tires and shit. Take it from me: living here makes your lungs complain." The chin-up bar remained idle during much of my tenure, because Stark, one time swinging back and forth and kicking himself up higher and higher, yanked one of the pipes from which it hung about four inches out of the ceiling. Both of us decided the set-up was too fragile to try any more chin-ups after that.

## *The Floor*

"Careful where you step!" Stark said as we began the Sangamon Tour. Heeding this warning of Stark's, I looked down and noticed floorboards bowing upwards throughout the loft, protruding nails more of a threat to ankles and feet than the prick of rattler fangs or lizard spines. Little did I know that one of many bad habits I picked up left of the Loop had begun: even today I stare at my feet whenever I take more than two steps. What started out as self-preserving watchfulness resulted in fishhook posture, which I ultimately attribute to rainwater seeping through gaps in our roof and warping the floor.

The floor of the loft was black, although it was hard to tell whether the color was due to paint; more likely the cause was soot, for coal granules coated every floorboard and filled every crack, reminder of a more primitive time when the building was heated by a coal furnace. When light struck it right, the floor sparkled, an effect I found unusual—one normally associates sparkles with cleanliness, not filth.

## *The Living Room*

The living room area was quite unremarkable; the only thing setting it apart from any other living room in America was the fact that a run-down loft surrounded it. Like every living room in America, its focal point was the TV. Beside the TV stood one of the posts necessary to support the ceiling. This post, being only one of three sources of power, was the locus of a spider web of electrical cords from the living room—its lights, stereo and TV. Also plugged into it was Stark's room, via an overloaded extension cord taped down to the floor with duct tape. Stark said my room would be plugged into this post, too. Last, he explained that the refrigerator plugged into this post, because the kitchen outlet could only carry the water heater, microwave oven, and bathroom. Like a fly buzzing dangerously close to a spider web, you had to watch yourself around the living room post, lest you become tangled up in the cords and invisible electrical filaments enshroud you.

Stark's living room furniture was second-hand and second-rate; no surprise here, since genuine Bauhaus or Memphis furniture, what people are accustomed to seeing in magazine pictures of lofts, certainly would be out of place at such a raw-boned loft. The sofa and love seat were given to Stark by his uncle; I'm torn between appreciating his gift, or being appalled at his taste. Though the two pieces matched, their color scheme consisted of an orange-brown background with a loud tan and red flower pattern, decoration that, regardless of the loft's decrepitude, would fit better in a vomitorium.

"Check out the Sangamon funk," Stark said, slapping one of the love seat's cushions. A veritable cumulonimbus cloud of dust rose up and enveloped the entire living room.

"You don't vacuum?" I asked.

"No vacuum cleaner."

"Cool," I said, then gave the sofa a thwack myself. Even though I owned a vacuum cleaner, I never once vacuumed up any Sangamon funk. We felt a perverse kind of pride in letting it gather where it might. Besides, in a matter of hours more funk would replace what you cleaned up earlier. And a good whap on the cushions and the resulting cloud effectively jolted anybody in the living room out of his or her dissipation.

The last words I want to say about the living room concern two pieces of furniture and how they symbolized our precarious existence: we had to watch how we set our beers on the end tables straddling the sofa, because the tabletops weren't attached to their barrel-like bases. If you weren't careful, you could flip the tabletop over, thereby plopping everything on the floor like a dropped spaghetti plate. Yet, despite our precautions, this unfortunate event occurred at least once a week.

## *The Drum Set*

Stark took me over to the corner where his band rehearsed. "Brand new set," he announced. "But I cracked the crash cymbal already." He spun the cymbal around to show me. "That little crack there doesn't look like much, but you don't get any give, like you're whacking tin." Similar to a new car owner, Stark was casting an appreciative eye on his set, but you could tell he was nettled at hearing a sound he didn't hear when things were new.

Stark's set truly was a plain one, the drum set of a minimalist: snare drum, bass drum, one side tom, one floor tom, and crash, ride and high-hat cymbals, what he called a "four-piece." Evidently, many drummers use a five-piece, with one extra side tom, and some use a dozen or more drums, adding "complexity" or "musical drumming" to their bands' music. Stark believed these drummers played too many notes; he preferred simply to keep the beat, considering that approach a more powerful one than playing the showy pomp and fanfare stuff.

The drum set always caught visitors' eyes first. Still standing in the doorway, with the big metal sliding steel door rolling back towards them, threatening to dislocate their left shoulders if they didn't jump aside, they craned their necks to catch a glimpse of it through the loft, just like they were straining to see a moose or deer hidden by trees in a forest. Every single visitor was spellbound by it, and, if Stark didn't intervene, he or she just might sit behind it, pick up a drumstick, and start tapping. Some visitors, mostly hangers-on accompanying musicians trying out for Stark's band, usually ex-drummers who quit in the eighth grade, but still the experts, were decidedly and vocally unimpressed. "You need more drums," they would say. In response, Stark mumbled something about the beauty of simplicity and soul, but really he wanted to yell, "Leave the drumming to me, you asshole backseat drummer!"

## *The Therapy Room*

My attention turned to a room in the northeast corner of the loft. "What's in here?" I asked. "Is this going to be my room?"

"I don't think you want to live in there. It's a pretty hostile environment." He opened the door, and I glanced inside. What I saw amazed me: filling the room from wall to wall there was an ankle-deep layer of broken glass. All that glass resembled a body of contaminated water; shattered brown and green bottles stirring among clear glass gave the room a muddy, stagnant look.

"I don't think I'd like to get thrown in there," I said.

"I call it the Therapy Room. It's a great place to blow off steam." He walked to the refrigerator, pulled out a bottle of orange juice, dumped its contents into the sink, then returned to the doorway. After winding up, he threw a strike at the wall, and glass splattered in every direction.

"You have any more bottles?" I asked, wanting to take my turn.

"Not right now. But if we get a twelve pack later, we'll save the empties and come over here to practice our throwing motions."

The Therapy Room was a hit with everyone we knew. More than once our friend Rick O'Shea stopped by carrying cardboard boxes full of beer bottles to fling. Apparently, Rick had an interest in glass that could be traced to his high school days; he told us that he used to take armfuls of bottles to a vacant lot, put on safety goggles, then smack them into oblivion with a baseball bat. Like pitchers at Wrigley Field pulling baseballs out of baskets and firing them in rapid succession while warming up, we threw hundreds of bottles at the wall. Suffice to say that Stark and I spent many happy hours in the Therapy Room relieving our overwrought and combative mental states.

## *The Bathroom*

Although not as primitive as an outhouse on a farm, the bathroom was backward by middle class standards, as I soon discovered when I needed to pay a visit. "Don't whiz in the urinal," Stark called through the door. "If you look underneath, you'll see that the drain pipe isn't connected anywhere. You'll whiz all over your shoes."

Heeding Stark's warning, I stepped up to the toilet and urinated. When finished, I examined the bathroom. Obviously, way back when, it was commonly shared by warehouse personnel. The urinal indicated this fact, as did the enclosed toilet stall, complete with a latchable door. Previous occupants since had tried to modify the room to suit more residential purposes, for an old-fashioned bathtub with legs was installed on an unpainted plywood platform about two feet off the floor. Leading up to the tub was a grimy step built by nailing boards together into a rectangular box.

To ensure privacy, someone had lined the windows with a speckled, translucent piece of cellophane. Though it gave a measure of privacy, its insulating properties were lacking. What I remember most about the bathroom was shivering from winter drafts after stepping out of the tub; to counteract the cold, we made a habit of taking our respective space heaters into the bathroom when we bathed.

Almost as aggravating, it took forever for the water heater to warm up enough water to fill the tub. Luckily, our bath times never overlapped, because it took a minimum of two hours for the water to warm sufficiently for a second person to bathe. Stark worked the day shift, so he took his bath in the morning, and I took my bath in the afternoon immediately before my shift, which started at five. Weekends sometimes presented a problem, however. Much more tolerant than the fastidious Stark, I usually waited for the appropriate interval to pass before taking my turn in the tub.

## *Stark's Room*

"I was always jealous of kids who had bunk beds," said Stark, taking me into his room. "You had a ladder to climb up if you slept in the top bunk. Now I have a ladder without the pain-in-the-butt little brother to go along with it." He had me climb up the ladder, which was constructed of two-by-fours, in order to peek into his sleeping loft.

"Why do you have a plastic cover over your mattress?" I asked.

"Because the water leaks in when it rains. Have to protect the mattress."

"Then why do you sleep up here?"

"It's the warmest spot in the loft. Heat rises, right? Look how far off the floor it is. It's got to be eight feet. I'd say it's ten degrees warmer than the rest of the loft up there."

"It reminds me of a crypt," I said, stepping back down the ladder and looking around me at the bedroom equivalent to a four-piece drum set: the only piece of furniture in the room was a dresser plastered with the ubiquitous notes Stark wrote to himself, plus a clock and a transistor radio.

## *My Room*

"I suppose we could sweep out all the glass and make the Therapy Room your room," said Stark. "But I'd rather not do that. How about sleeping in here," he suggested, opening the door to what amounted to a walk-in closet.

"I think my bed will fit in here," I said. "And I don't have much of anything else coming on the truck. This ought to be fine." When I left the west, I decided to discard all my worldly possessions; except for my bed and a few other odds and ends, I bequeathed everything to my previous roommate, a guy known around town as Scary Larry.

A week after my arrival, when the moving van dropped off what remained of my stuff, I set out to appoint my room. I kept all my underwear and socks in a suitcase, and I hung my shirts and pants from nails pounded into the studs. I pushed my old twin bed against the wall. A ratty old rug on which I slept during naptime in kindergarten completed the ensemble. All in all it was a Spartanly comfortable room.

There was one problem, though. The ceiling to my room, really a sub-ceiling far below the ceiling to the rest of the loft, was a crude one made of masonite sheets whose gaps allowed glass to trickle in. Each morning when I rose from bed I would carefully place my feet on the floor after a quick feel-around with my big toe, hoping I wouldn't step on any glass shards.

You see, bottle throwing wasn't exclusively limited to the Therapy Room. Stark had a habit, during TV commercials featuring histrionic car dealership owners he didn't like, of yelling "Get the hell off my TV!" and throwing any handy glass container onto the box-like enclosure.

Sometimes the bottles broke, causing glass to rain down upon the living room, sometimes not. "I like the delicious agony of not knowing if they'll pop," he explained once, "hoping they do, but kind of hoping they don't." In the middle of the night, shards of glass would slip between cracks and flowed down the walls on the inside of my room like a glass waterfall. It was this glass my feet wanted to avoid.

Unable to shake Stark out of this behavior, because it was an instinctive thing, not anything he thought about, I soon became accustomed to it like I became accustomed to all of the other perils of living on Sangamon Street. I figured that if Stark could take water flooding his sleeping quarters, I could handle a little broken glass in mine.

****

What I saw of my new home jogged my memory of earlier experiences living with Stark. When we met five years before as roommates in a college dormitory, Stark caused several hundred dollars' worth of damage to our room. One time, he set a fire in the middle of our floor; in the process, he melted fourteen floor tiles. Another time, he slammed the door to our room so hard that the doorway, frame and everything, tore out of the wall and crashed into the hallway.

After that incident, he and I were kicked out of the dorm, so we moved to an off-campus apartment. While walking there from the bar one drunken night, I found myself toting off a tollway sign, including the twelve-foot metal pole, which I found uprooted beside the road. Since Stark's birthday was that same week, I gave him the sign as a gift. He proceeded to lob it around the living room, enjoying particularly the gigantic BANG! when it hit the floor. A few nights later he got the idea he was Sir Lancelot—he tucked the pole under his arm and went jousting. The next morning we counted sixty-seven holes jabbed into the walls.

"Looks like you've finally hit on a place that's completely Stark-proof," I said after my tour, looking approvingly at the loft overall and its solid brick walls.

"Yeah, finally," he answered.

# 2 | Total Strangers: Part One

Within a couple of weeks of moving into Stark's loft, I had a job; my title was Night Proofreader at a law firm in the Loop called Sickly & Caustic. Even though the firm represented some loathsome clients like Megadump Waste Disposal Corporation and the Trans-Demonic Phone System, I accepted the job, figuring I could quit later when I had a record of work experience in Chicago. Plus, given my academic background, Sickly looked like the only place that would offer me employment at the time.

Because I worked the night shift, nearly two months passed before I was able to witness a rehearsal, one Sunday, of Stark's band, The Strangers. The band usually practiced on Tuesday and Thursday nights, but they all recently had decided to add Sunday as a rehearsal night, because, according to Stark, they agreed they needed to improve quite a bit if they wanted to play some gigs at local bars during the coming spring.

"We need to find a steady lead guitarist, too," he said. "We're trying out another guy tonight. Our last one—what was his name?—was in the band for less than a month."

"Guitar players are a dime a dozen," I said.

"Rudy the Roach is bringing along a lead singer, too, which is cool, because his voice isn't so hot. It cracks all the time because he smokes so much."

"Rudy the Roach plays rhythm guitar?"

“Yeah, and he writes the songs. He’s a great songwriter. I’m worried about this singer he’s bringing, though. Her name’s Wanda. She’s his new girlfriend. Just because she’s his girlfriend doesn’t mean she’ll be any good. The two don’t automatically follow.”

“Have you met her?”

“Yeah. At Rudy’s place. Before she moved to Chicago she was a model in New York. Rudy says if we have a pretty face fronting us, that’ll be a plus, because there are so many goons out there singing in bands. But can she sing?”

“You haven’t heard her?”

“No, so far she’s only been rehearsing with Rudy so she’ll learn the songs.”

“I’m glad I finally got the chance to hear this band you’re playing in. I’m really looking forward to it.”

“I’m not promising anything.”

We heard a car door slam outside. Stark ran out the doorway and down the stairs to open the street door, for we lacked such luxuries as a doorbell or a buzzer to let people in our door. When we expected visitors, we listened for their car door to slam or for them to yell up at our windows. One of us then had to go downstairs to open the door.

A minute or so later, a short, skinny man dragged a woman quite a bit taller than him by her wrist through the door. He carried a guitar case in his other hand. “I want to know. I want to KNOW!” the woman said, verging on the hysterical.

“Into the bathroom. Into the BATHROOM!” the guy shouted back.

“Let GO of me,” she responded. The two wrestled for a few seconds, which caused the guitar case to swing around and slam into our groty old gas heater. Soot fluttered down from where the stovepipe joined the ceiling.

Stark followed this display, shaking his head while walking over to the living room. The two wrestlemaniacs turned the corner and grappled their way into the bathroom, punching and thrashing all the while. The guy slammed the door behind them.

"This could go on for an hour," Stark said. "When I was over at Rudy's last week, they suddenly erupted into an argument and locked themselves in the bathroom. I watched TV for half an hour, and then I got up to leave. When I left they were still in there, yelling and screaming and shit."

"Looks like band practice will be a little late."

"Looks like."

"Why do you call him 'Rudy the Roach?'"

"He told me he used to be a junkie, so I figure he's developed the physical constitution of a cockroach. Watch how he scoots and flits around the loft."

Somebody turned up the volume knob on our bathroom. "I won't ask again," said the woman. "Where did you spend the night last night?"

"Look, you don't own me," said the man.

"I SLEEP with you! Isn't that enough?" Suddenly the woman stormed out of the bathroom; sniffling and rubbing her eyes, she walked over to the big sliding steel door and struggled with it for a moment. Unable to open it right away, she yelled "FUCK!" and then she kicked it. The force of her blow caused the door to reverberate like a gong. She finally succeeded at sliding it out of her way, and we heard the stamping sound of her feet slowly fade as she descended the stairs.

A moment or two later, Rudy the Roach poked his head out from behind the bathroom door. "The coast is clear," Stark yelled in response to Rudy's tentativeness. Rudy came full out of the bathroom and paused at the window, looking down at the street.

"She's down sitting on the curb, pouting to herself," he said. He turned and walked over to join Stark and me in the living room area. Glancing back at the window and pointing at it with his thumb, he said, "Don't worry; she'll be back. I've got the car keys." He pulled his keys out of his pocket and showed them to us, jangling them for effect.

"Say, you must be the redoubtable Ishmael Spungkdt. The name's Rudy," he said.

"Call me Ish," I said.

"What do you think of my man Stark's humble abode?" he asked me.

"It's okay."

"It sure does bring back memories. It's like I was at the factory all over again."

"The factory? You're getting nostalgic about working in a factory?" I asked.

"No, no. *The Factory*," he said. "You know—Andy Warhol's loft."

"You've been to Andy Warhol's loft?" I asked.

"Sure. I used to hang out there all the time. I was a real youngster when I first got there, a real snot-nosed kid. I just moved to New York from my hometown, Hibbing, Minnesota. That's where Bob Dylan's from, you know."

"Yeah, I know," I said. "Sounds like you knew Andy pretty well."

"You know how some people collect stamps or coins? Well, Andy collected people. That was his trip, the voyeuristic bastard. We'd all get strung out on speed or junk, and he'd just sit there like he was the master chemist or something, watching our chemicals mix and waiting for side effects. I partied with some real spaced-out cats like Edie Sedgwick, Viva, Ultra Violet, Candy Darling the transvestite, Paul Morrissey, Lou Reed. He was with the Velvet Underground, you know."

"Yeah, I know." I looked at Stark, but he wasn't listening. He was busy reading a *Rolling Stone* magazine.

"I was even there the day Andy got shot. When they were wheeling him out on a stretcher, I walked along and held his hand, and I kept whispering in his ear, over and over, 'You're gonna make it, man. You're gonna make it.' I thought I'd never see him again, because his stomach was bleeding so bad, but damn him if he didn't pull through."

"Sounds pretty glamorous," I said.

"You could say it was. He had a good place. But there were plenty of coldwater places in New York at the time, too. Places that make your loft look like the Drake Hotel. I remember one loft I used to flop at. A bunch of hippies squatted there and ran it like a commune. If you didn't have a place to stay, or if you wanted to score some dope, you could go there, and if you looked freaky enough, they took you in. The whole damn place was full of bunk beds. There might be a hundred and fifty hippies sleeping there on any given night."

"You were a hippie?"

"Sure. You wouldn't believe it looking at what a short hair I am now, but back in '68 and '69 I had the whole shebang—long hair, love beads, tie-dyed jeans, everything. Anyway, I woke up there one morning, and somebody was in bed with me. This wasn't very unusual back in those days, but when I rose up to see who it was, I couldn't believe my eyes. It was Allen Ginsberg, sucking on my dick!"

"You're kidding."

"No, man, scout's honor."

"Sounds like you've been around." Actually, it sounded to me like he was full of shit. But then again, maybe not, because when I sneaked a look at the insides of his arms, I saw the collapsed veins which verified the fact that at some prior time in his life he was a needle user. Maybe he truly did shoot up with the Warhol crowd. In any case, the stories that he told to Stark and me during the two years we knew him covered two decades of counterculture legends and lore. In addition to the names he dropped the first time we met, at later Rudy the Roach story hours he claimed to have hung around with:

Laurie Anderson
Lester Bangs
Ted Berrigan
Paul Bowles
William Burroughs

David Byrne
John Cale
Jim Carroll
Bob Dylan
Brian Eno
John Giorno
Debbie Harry
Richard Hell
David Johannssen
Lenny Kaye
Phil Ochs
Yoko Ono
Joey Ramone
Johnny Ramone
Dee Dee Ramone
Jerry Rubin
Ed Sanders
Sam Shepard
Patti Smith
Chris Stein
Tom Verlaine
Suzanne Vega

"Do you mind if I ask you a question? How old are you?" I asked.

"How old do you think I am?"

"You look 29 or 30."

"Thanks for the compliment. Actually, I'm almost 40. You ever hear of William Burroughs?"

"Uh, yeah. I read my first book of his, *Naked Lunch*, when I was 16."

"I was 14. Anyway, Burroughs wrote in one of his books, and I can't remember right now which one, that doing junk has this suspended animation effect. He was referring to these experiments that scientists did on worms. They soaked the worms in pure heroin, and they found the heroin slowed down their metabolism so much that they could live ten times longer than normal. I guess you could say I'm pretty well preserved from junk."

He cracked his knuckles and stretched. "I'm going downstairs to check on Wanda," he said. He got up from the couch and left Stark and me to ourselves.

"Boing! Boing! Boing!" I said.

"What's that for?" asked Stark.

"That's the bouncing sound of all those names he dropped. I'm sorry, but those stories he just told us are pretty hard to believe."

"I don't know what to believe. I know he's from New York. I know he was a junkie once. After awhile I tune him out."

"Now I see why you call him 'Rudy the Roach,'" I said.

"He's a survivor. He's like a cockroach that lived through a nuclear war and lived to tell about it," said Stark.

At this point, Rudy returned with Wanda; they now were holding hands, this time voluntarily. She kissed him on the cheek, let go of his hand, then proceeded to wander around the loft, looking around. She didn't seem at all intimidated by the place, which was a refreshing change from most visitors, most of whom found excuses to leave in a hurry, but rather she acted curious, like a dog put in a new, unfamiliar yard, eagerly sniffing out every fencepost and tree.

After she took a turn around the loft, she ended up in the living room area with Rudy, Stark and me. Like nearly everybody else who took the loft tour, she ended up at the climax of the tour, the "Kill Your Pets" graffiti.

This was a piece of artwork recently spraypainted on the wall by an acquaintance I made, a genuine artist (as opposed to us spraypaint doodlers), who had shown her work in galleries over on Superior Street. Her work mostly reflected her grotesque fascination with dead or dying animals—gophers getting ripped open by hawks, run over cats with squashed hindquarters, that kind of thing. "Kill Your Pets" was no exception to this theme.

The picture consisted of a pointy-eared, cartoony dog with a turquoise face atop a silver body being run through by a spear. Naturally, my friend sprayed lots of red paint around the poor dog's wound all close-like so the appropriate dribbling and spurting blood effects were achieved. Around this scene, she painted a background of fluorescent orange, a real eye-catching color to say the least. She topped off the picture, like all of her dead animal pictures, with a prominent textual message: "Kill Your Pets." What I found truly striking about her picture was the dog's eyes. They had this look of glassing over, not of eyes already glassed over, but in the *process* of glassing over, like the dog's death was perpetually in progress. I really admired her skill in creating this effect with a clumsy can of spraypaint instead of a teeny little paintbrush that lesser artists would require. She even dated her picture and signed it, thus supplying a pair of culture-starved roommates with an original artwork, one we were proud to have on display in our living room.

Anyway, Wanda stared at the picture for a bit, tilting her head this way and that, then turned around and said, "This place is so *Bohemian*! It's so . . . so *New York*!"

"Except there ain't no boutiques on Sangamon," said Stark, a tinge annoyed at the comparison.

"He's right, Wanda" Rudy said. "Remember this is Chicago, not New York. You know, the city of big shoulders. The city with the biggest chips on the biggest shoulders."

Wanda playfully punched Rudy's arm, then began to sing arpeggios, evidently as warm-up for the practice that didn't seem would ever get started. She always was flat on the dominant, and each time she approached it, I winced.

About seven or eight arpeggios later, we heard a car honk repeatedly outside. Stark went downstairs; he returned with two more guys carrying guitar cases. "Got off at the wrong place. I thought there was an exit off the expressway for Halsted," one announced. "Then we drove all over downtown. If I hadn't've seen that 'Yes Sir, Senator' place, and known how to get here from there, we'd still be driving around." In this last bit, he was referring to the signs on Barney's Market Club over on the corner of Randolph and Halsted.

"Spungkdt, Danny. Danny, Spungkdt," Rudy said, introducing us. "Danny plays bass."

"Welcome to Sangamon Street," I said.

"Killer place, dude," the other new guy said to Stark, setting down his guitar and pulling off his down-filled ski vest.

Stark sat behind his drums and kicked the bass drum pedal a couple of times. "Let's get this practice on the road," he said.

"Those are all the drums you have, dude?" the guitarist asked, looking over Stark's drum set.

"Yeah, I play a four piece."

"You dudes really go for the primitive here."

"It's livable once you get the hang of it. Always wear shoes so you won't get glass in your foot. Never take a bath less than two hours after somebody else so there'll be hot water. Shit like that."

"Sure, dude. Anything you say. Is it okay to piss anywhere, or do you dudes have a can?"

"Over there."

"Thanks, dude." The guitarist went into the bathroom, and Rudy walked over and began unpacking his guitar.

"I see you met Eric," Rudy said.

"Where did you get that guy from?" asked Stark.

"The ad in last week's *Illinois Entertainer*. He was the only one who called. Danny had to drive out to Downers Grove to pick him up."

"He's got about as much personality as a glass of tap water."

"Give him a chance. Maybe he'll be enlightened if we apply a little Zentron to him."

"Zentron?" asked Stark.

Upon hearing this word, I went into the closet and dug out a can of red spraypaint. To the left of Stark's drums I spraypainted the word "Zentron" on the wall. "Stand him under that," I said. "Maybe it'll sink in."

"Let's all of us tune up," said Rudy, now that Eric, Danny and Wanda had gathered in the band area. The three guitarists strapped on their guitars and proceeded to tune up. Wanda attempted more arpeggios in the key they were tuning to, but she still was a shade flat on that pesky dominant.

Rudy passed a sheet of paper over to Eric. "Those are the changes. Listen to Danny and me for the groove, and I'll tell you when to come in for your solos."

"No problem, dude."

With that they kicked into the first song. I grabbed a chair and sat myself in front of them to watch. Stark was right; Rudy's music was very well written. It generally was upbeat, and full of some memorable hooks. Plus all the players' amps were set at a nicely rude garage band level, which was appropriate, since the loft, if it were set on the first floor, would be indistinguishable from a garage. And of course it was a thrill seeing Stark thumping away at the drums with a band around him, rather than by himself like I was accustomed.

After a couple of songs that duly impressed me, Rudy called for a break. Everybody except Wanda huddled in the living room to smoke a joint that Rudy pulled out of his shirt pocket. Wanda took a *Glamour* magazine into the bathroom with her.

"Wanda doesn't get high?" I asked, passing the joint Rudy passed to me over to Stark.

"Not anymore," said Rudy. "She used to hang out with a pretty bent crowd, modeling agency and music promoter types, and she got all strung out on coke. That's why she left New York, to get away from them. It's too bad, too, because she just started singing and a promoter put her in a band, and she did a video that they showed on MTV."

"What was the band?" I asked.

"They were called The Flirts. It was an all-girl band."

"I remember the video. But it's been so long, I don't remember her being in it."

"It didn't get very much airplay. You probably never heard from them after that, because when she left I think the band broke up."

"I remember that video," Eric said. "It was *awesome*. HEY, WANDA!" he yelled in the direction of the bathroom, "you were awesome in the Flirts video."

"Thank you," she yelled back.

Unfortunately, I didn't share Eric's enthusiasm for Wanda's video. What I remember of it were scenes with these three women singers strutting down the street looking real mean and bitchy like the models in women's magazines do these days—you know, not one smile in the bunch, just real hard-ass sneers. I remember thinking at the time that this was no band in the traditional sense, but a bunch of models somebody collected together to make a video, most likely with dubbed-in voices. MTV only recently had gone on the air, and being in its nascent phase (they didn't even air commercials in the early days), I figured they probably had a difficult time scratching together quality videos.

Tipsy from Rudy's joint, the four instrumentalists returned to the band area. Rudy called to Wanda that they were ready to go again. "Not yet," she yelled, still in the bathroom. "I've got to finish this article first. It's about PMS. You know what a nightmare that can be."

"Article? C'mon! It's almost ten o'clock," Rudy said.

About five minutes later, Wanda came out. When she brushed by me as I sat in my chair waiting through the band's interminable delays, I caught a whiff of her. You'd think that an ex-model would pay scrupulous attention to every detail of her dress and personal grooming, but Wanda very definitely neglected the latter I immediately discovered. Rather than smelling perfume like you would expect of a model, I smelled a gamy sort of smell emanating from her, one that called to mind fresh-skinned beaver pelts, although, admittedly, I've never in my life smelled beaver pelts.

During the break, Stark hauled over the ladder he snatched from upstairs when he first moved to Sangamon, and he screwed in blue and red light bulbs into the sockets above the band area. The colored lights created a nightclub atmosphere, and as I sat in my chair, I thought how lucky I was. Most people had to go out to experience the night life, pay cover charges, buy expensive, watered-down drinks, and put up with drunks, well-dressed drunks to be sure, but drunks nonetheless. Whereas with me, living left of the Loop, the nightlife came to my house. So there I sat in the Sangamon Nightclub, legs crossed, relaxing with a cigarette and a beer, entertained by live music other people would have to pay money to see.

When the band kicked into the next few songs, I inspected Wanda more closely. She sure was a good choice, looks-wise, with her cute, rounded face and full lips that dabbed the microphone as she sang. On that first night she wore a very tight, flesh-colored body suit that revealed a somewhat bony body—her shoulder, hip and tailbones poked through. I like women who are a bit more stacked, but I could forgive Wanda her skinny build, for that was the feminine ideal promulgated by models shown on TV, in magazines, everywhere. Her body suit also revealed vague maroon circles atop her breasts; when I noticed this, sexual soup began to simmer in my lap.

This soup gradually cooled off, however, when I took a close look at how she moved and listened carefully to how she sang. She seemed to have trouble keeping her balance, like her feet were nailed to the floor, and she didn't appear to have much of a sense of rhythm—she bounced and waved her arms either a little behind the beat or a lot ahead of the next beat. This gawkiness seemed out of place for a model, somebody you would expect to possess all kinds of grace and poise. Maybe she didn't spend enough time walking around with books on her head in charm school.

I've already mentioned Wanda's inability to hit certain notes in the arpeggios she sang; this difficulty with intonation carried through in the songs she sang with the band. This is not good when you consider that rock and roll utilizes only three or four chords, and features melodies that usually emphasize the tonic and dominant. So if you can't hit that dominant straight on, you're in trouble. She also sang kind of half-heartedly. This was most evident when between songs she dragged over a chair from our living room area and sat down, singing from a droopy sitting position for the rest of the night. Several of Rudy's more frenetic songs required the singer to belt out the lyrics, even scream. After an especially hollow screaming performance, Rudy stopped the song.

"You have to scream from the gut. Scream like you just got shot in the gut," he demanded of her.

"I'm tired," she said. "It's time to go." It looked like she barely could keep her eyelids up.

"No, it's not time to go; we still have time to run through another few songs."

"YOU'RE ALWAYS PICKING ON ME!" she exploded, screaming the best she screamed all night. Then she heaved the microphone stand onto the floor, causing shrill, ear-piercing feedback, after which she stomped into the bathroom where she stayed for the rest of the rehearsal.

"Let's start over. I'll sing for now," Rudy said to the rest of the band. He picked up the microphone stand and stood it upright, thus squelching the feedback tearing open my head. He lit up a cigarette, took a weary drag, and tucked it under a tuning peg on the neck of his guitar. During the guitar solos, when Eric flailed away on his Stratocaster, Rudy stuck his cigarette between his teeth and yelled directions through it, much like a traffic cop with his whistle.

"Eleven, two, three, four. Twelve, two, three, four. Thirteen, two, three, four. Hold it! Eric, you've got to solo over sixteen more bars of rhythm guitar. The solo is thirty-two bars long."

"This is the second guitar solo of the song, dude. I've run out of ideas."

"A guitar stud like yourself shouldn't have any problems coming up with thirty-two bars of solo guitar. Stretch it out."

"Sure thing, dude."

To save time they started at the second guitar solo. For twelve bars or so, Eric's fingers flew up and down the neck of his guitar as he played piles and piles of chromatic runs punctuated with whammy bar bends. He truly was a fast guitarist the way he crammed notes into every available space. But then he just petered out after a few more bars. Rudy growled at him through the cigarette clenched between his teeth, but he didn't stop the song. If it's true what guitarists say, that playing guitar is like making love to a woman, then Eric's guitar would have been left unsatisfied. Following this metaphor through to its logical conclusion, you could say that his solo amounted to a premature ejaculation.

"Okay, okay. Let's pack up and call it a night," Rudy sighed when the song was done. The guitar players rubbed down their guitars with rags, and put them in their cases. When Eric and Danny got up to leave, Rudy invited Eric back for the next rehearsal. When Stark heard this, he shot a nasty scowl Rudy's way.

"The plan is we rehearse the whole spring. We put together a demo tape that'll get us into some of the clubs. We get a little club exposure during the next year or two, say at the Avalon and the Cubby Bear and the West End. Then we go into the studio and record another demo that we'll send off to a major label. With Wanda fronting us it's a cinch we'll go national inside of three years."

"Thanks, but no thanks, dude. You've got some great originals, but there's no buckos playing for the crowds you're talking about. I think I'm gonna try and hook up with a top forty band and play down on Rush Street where the real bucks are. Good meeting all you dudes." With that, he and Danny left.

"Looks like I have to run another ad," Rudy said.

"Face it, Rudy, he was a mindless suburban chopster," said Stark. "We need somebody like Ron Wood to play rock and roll, not this fast-finger, Paganini shit."

"He couldn't sustain much of a solo anyway," said Rudy. "Well, let me see if I can get Wanda out of the bathroom." A minute later, they walked out, arm in arm, with Rudy walking on tiptoes, whispering soothing words up into her ear. Neither bothered to say good-bye.

"What do you think?" asked Stark.

"An interesting bunch to be sure," I said.

"I haven't made up my mind about them yet. Rudy sure talks like he's got big plans and that he's serious, but with all these Wanda tantrums, I don't know."

"She *is* a bit high-strung. Pretty though."

"Give her some training in solfege, and she could fake her way through a song pretty well," said Stark.

"You ought to suggest she take some singing lessons."

"I'll leave that to Rudy. You saw her. She doesn't take criticism so well. Let me ask you this: what did you think of Rudy's songwriting?"

"Honestly? I'd say the hooks and riffs and lyrics are first rate. But I don't know about all those guitar solos. I thought at first that Dudesickle, or whatever his name was, kept peaking too soon. He himself said he ran out of ideas. But now that I think about it, I get the impression that Rudy's songs are all about eighty-eight bars too long. He could write these snappy three-minute pop songs, but he puts five guitar solos into every tune, so you turn out having a ten minute song."

"That's what the audience wants. They want a guitarist to spell everything out for them, to paint all the corners. It's because they haven't got the imagination to paint the corners themselves."

"I see. Still, you have to have some space, some breathing room."

"I know what you mean, but it's Rudy's decision because they're his songs."

"Say, there's something that bothers me about Wanda," I said. "If she used to be this glamorous model in New York, why is she so unkempt? She looked like she hadn't combed her hair in weeks, and she had these stains down the front of her body suit."

"I guess she doesn't have anybody pampering her anymore. You know how models have somebody behind the scenes who does their hair and dresses them? She doesn't have that."

"I noticed she smelled pretty funky, too. Come to think of it, Rudy had this vague chili pepper smell himself."

"I figured that out. They don't shower real often 'cause they associate body odor with being 'Continental.' It's like they can act all Continental and worldly without ever leaving Chicago."

It was past eleven, and Stark retired to his room for the night. Wired from the night's events, I began picking up the twenty-five or so cigarette butts which Rudy the Roach ground out with his shoe and left on the floor in the band area. "Why didn't he use the damn ashtray?" I mumbled to myself. "This may only be a crappy loft, but it's still my home."

# 3 Food and Diet

"Did I tell you about the other night when I was seriously dissipated?" Stark asked me one Saturday afternoon. "I was too dissipated to boil noodles for macaroni and cheese, so I ate a bowl-full of bacon bits and drank two Pepsis in a row really fast. They were the most accessible things to eat. I didn't feel too good a little while later, though."

This anecdote of Stark's got me thinking about our diets on Sangamon. Despite Stark's mad consumption of bacon bits, our wolfing down of two or three bags of nacho cheese-flavored Dorito chips during football games on TV, or the ritualistic Sunday morning Cap'n Crunch binges, all told we had a pretty healthy time of it food-wise, for we lived smack in the middle of Chicago's largest wholesale food market.

Immediately west of Haymarket Square, just to the south of us, a string of fresh fruit and vegetable businesses straddled Randolph Street from Halsted to Racine. Every morning, trucks exited off the Dan Ryan expressway via the Randolph Street ramp, then parked under the awnings of individual produce stands. Each trailer contained loads of produce picked at truck farms in the surrounding region during summer, or winter vegetables transferred to trucks from refrigerator cars hauled out of California by rail. This system of transportation combined with our own happy location adjacent to the marketplace resulted in our eating the freshest, cheapest greens available in Chicago. And, as my mother always told me, greens are good for the body, mechanically as well as chemically.

Even though Stark and I didn't own a restaurant or a mom and pop grocery, and therefore should have appeared like small potatoes in their eyes, the produce sellers tolerated our presence well enough, especially at our favorite place, Karos' Produce Stand, on the corner of Randolph and Green. The old man's son, Andy, always fell all over himself dropping the fruits and vegetables I picked out into little brown paper bags, weighing them on his scale, then saying "six bucks" while holding up six fingers. And there were many afternoons I stopped on my walk to work to pick out an apple to go in my sack lunch, when, more often than not, the old man himself wouldn't charge me anything. Such was the friendly, generous Karos family.

Vegetables bought from Karos' Produce Stand provided us with a veritable salad bar of items to toss in our salads. We chose from a crisper full of carrots, broccoli, cauliflower, bean sprouts, pea pods, celery, tomatoes, and three different kinds of lettuce. Then we doused our salads with a special house dressing, a pukey, orange-colored concoction made from left-over French, Thousand Island, Ranch and oil and vinegar dressings, stored in a mayonnaise jar.

A half-block north of the loft was Fulton Market, headquarters in the city for wholesale meat. Carl Sandburg once called Chicago "Hog Butcher for the World." I'm witness that this no longer is the case; rather, Chicago should be called "Middleman of the World." The stockyards have long been shut down, so most of the pork and beef that arrived around the corner was already butchered in Topeka and Omaha, evidenced by the big semis that rolled up revealing license plates from Kansas or Nebraska. Up and down Fulton Street were dozens of packinghouses taking delivery from these trucks of sides of beef, skinned pigs, crates of chickens and even eggs.

On summer days I used to sit on the sidewalk across the street from our loft and sun myself on what we called the

"Sangamon Beach," where I studied the meat packing business that surrounded me. Most apparent were the semis that periodically rolled to a halt right in front of me, forcing me to move my chair further down the block out of their shadows. I considered these trucks a menace, because they sat idling in the street, expelling truck fumes into the air, sometimes for hours at a time, before backing into the docks. Certain afternoons when the air was heavy with humidity, I'd look up at our windows and swear I saw truck fumes slither in the cracks of window frames, like the Angel of Death fog that crept under Pharaoh's door in the movie *The Ten Commandments*.

Less threatening to your health, but definitely more horrifying when you saw the sight, were the multitudes of meatpackers in bloodied white aprons wheeling around cardboard drums filled to the brim with bones and guts, which they poured into dumpsters. After about three p.m., when all the meat packers vacated the neighborhood, thus leaving Sangamon Street more quiet and still than a ghost town, I used to see parades of bums carrying away three or four empty drums slung over their shoulders, off to Peterson Barrel Company, on the corner of Monroe and Green, which paid cash to anyone who recovered these drums in an undamaged condition. If you turned in a barrel with tin metal rings still capping its ends, then you received fifty cents; if the metal rings were missing, you were paid fifty cents for two.

A local landmark always looming over the Sangamon Beach, doing its own part in blotting out the sun, was the Fulton Market Cold Storage building, the largest structure by far in the immediate vicinity, a building so tall it could be seen all the way from the Loop. We used to walk through the shadow it made, no matter what time of day, on our way to wash clothes in the Puerto Rican neighborhood north of Grand Avenue. Beyond being big, it gave off a high-pitched, electronic glissando sound every few seconds. It went "Eeeeoop. Eeeeoop. Eeeeoop." Stark, always the neighborhood booster, pronounced Fulton Market Cold Storage

"Our answer to the Merchandise Mart." In any case, this building was an impressive monument dedicated to the meatpacking industry; it would have made Sandburg proud, even with the demise of the stockyards.

Perhaps the best reminder of the neighborhood's character and purpose was what Stark and I called the "bone chute." A fiberglass device sticking out of a wall of the packinghouse across the street, the bone chute's conveyer belt ferried the spinal columns, skulls, rib cages and pelvises of countless slaughtered cattle into the back of a dump truck parked underneath. All day long the bones, still red with flesh, would drop into the truck; with each thud, the truck bed echoed through Sangamon Street like an over-sized bass drum. Then, promptly at three, the truck would pull out, empty its bones somewhere, and return for the next day's load. Although curious, we never found out where the bones were shipped. Perhaps they were taken to a dog food factory, where they were ground up into the bone meal dog food cans say they contain.

It became a point of pride for Stark and me to limit our meat intake to what was prepared and packaged in the same zip code as we lived in, 60607. Though when you walked by the Ball Park Franks factory it smelled like giblet gravy was simmering inside, we still ate their hot dogs, for sentimental reasons as well as for convenience: we had heard since we were kids the slogan "They plump when you cook them" on the radio during Cubs games. Another local specialty was gyros; we bought gyros meat from a wholesale operation down Fulton Street displaying a sign that advertised "Fresh Killed Lambs." We served it on pita bread, along with sour cream, tomatoes, onions, and olives fished out of brine-filled barrels at Karos' Produce Stand.

A typical dish of Stark's, one he liked so much that he ate it twelve or fifteen nights in a row, was baked chicken, which he buried with so much Lowry's seasoning salt that the pan looked like a sandbox. But, though he loved his chicken, by far his favorite dinner was grilled sausage, a seasonal treat. Given the time, a westerly wind and the right mood, Stark would roll his old, battered Weber grill out onto our stairway landing and fire it up. While sausage sizzled away on his grill, we both worked up an appetite waving our arms to chase smoke out the window. We sampled a number of types of sausage on these occasions—Polish sausage, Italian sausage, chorizo, kielbasa, bratwurst, hot dogs or lamb sausage—whatever he found on sale after scouting Fulton Market's butcher shops.

Lest the reader worry about sanitary conditions where the meat on his or her table was packaged, I can assure you that every day armies of men hosed down the docks and sidewalks with a chlorine-smelling solution. I'm quite certain such clean-up operations were conducted inside the packinghouses as well. Nonetheless, I was never brave enough to read *The Jungle* while I lived and ate left of the Loop.

# 4 Philosophical Roots of Outer Bohemia

A rawboned loft stuck in the heart of the Near West Side just north of Skid Row along Madison Street, a part of town that had seen better (and worse) days, our home was forty-eight hundred square feet of space which Stark and I constantly re-shaped according to the dictates of our imaginations. The neighborhood was, without rhyme or reason, where we landed, a place whose amenities our eyes had to carve from cavernous warehouses, vacant lots, abandoned railroad spurs and cobble-stone streets turned up by weeds. While our eyes transformed the cityscape, our insides transformed as well; we created a mental landscape and we invented ourselves thereby.

Who I am, or who I invented myself as, owes a lot to living left of the Loop. One theory I have is that my behavior while living there was, well, childlike. (Most people would probably call it child*ish*.) In my defense against all so-called adults in the world, I will quote Wordsworth, who wrote, "The Child is Father of the man." Looked at his way, you could say that I was continuing my boyhood days by camping out on Sangamon Street.

When I was nine or ten, I used to gather with various friends at a train crossing roughly halfway between the two fairly close villages where we all lived. We rode our Schwinn Sting Rays up blacktop roads to this spot, which was along the Burlington

Northern line. East was Chicago; west eventually took you to Denver. About a half-mile down the tracks there was a trestle that spanned Blackberry Creek.

Heading toward this trestle, we tiptoed on the rails pretending we walked a tightrope; if we lost our balance, we let out the appropriate trailing-off scream of a man falling to his death, just like we heard on TV. Underneath the trestle we bombed pop cans with rocks, trying to sink them before the brown current of the creek carried them off. When we felt especially daredevilish, we would sidestep across the trestle, feet on a side girder holding the structure up, hands gripping the ties just inches from the rails.

The danger this stunt involved was two-fold: first, in case a train came along, you couldn't go anywhere but down into the water twenty-five feet below; second, danger could arise later if you survived creeping across the trestle, but your dad spotted creosote on your good winter coat. Creosote could be avoided if we were careful, and we thought we had the train covered: if the signal two miles down the tracks shone green, we knew a train would come within five minutes.

Feeling the delicious rumbling grow beneath our feet, we would quit our play to watch the train thunder past. We always waved to the engineer, who leaned out of his cab to wave back. Then we watched as its string of cars clickety-clacked past. We didn't merely count the number of freight cars in the train like other kids; instead, we looked at the logos of the various railroads represented in the train. If a train were made up of cars from the Santa Fe, Southern Pacific, Western Pacific, Union Pacific, or Rio Grande, we knew it was going to California, either to San Francisco or Los Angeles. If, on the other hand, there were mostly cars from the Milwaukee Road, Chicago Northwestern, or Canadian Pacific, or if it was a piggyback train saddled with either containers or trailers, we knew that it would take the northwest route up to Seattle.

It was then that I would regret not being somewhere on that train, maybe in a high-cube boxcar surrounded by auto parts rolling through the California desert, or in one of the containers which eventually would be shipped out of Puget Sound and off to Japan.

When I moved to the city at age eleven, I still had the itch to ride my bicycle somewhere else than to nearby parks and playgrounds, which I found way too tame. So I followed the rails into manufacturing districts, where I would dodge trucks, forklifts, mud puddles and bumpy sets of train sidings in the path of my bicycle's wheels. I remember listening to all the factory sounds, all the "whoop whoop whoops," the "ZZZ ZZZs," the "whim! whams!" and the "thunk-thunk-thunk-thunk-thunks" that I knew I liked, but wondered why, since most kids I knew liked the sounds of wind, waves, birds and the local high school's fight song.

While living left of the Loop, I recognized that these sounds were the percussion section which, continuing into the present, accompanied my own particular march to a different drummer.

From time to time, I walked along the train tracks octopussing around my West Loop neighborhood, my own private playground, in order to clear my head of the same old things haunting me: arguments with my dad, encounters with bullies, other awkward episodes that mark the coming of age. Nothing much had changed from my childhood, except when signals turned green, I had less than a minute until some cold, steel commuter train came roaring through. Of course, common sense said that climbing on the elevated tracks was out, because of the frequency with which the trains clattered by, not to mention the third rail electrifying the line, which would have been a mistake to brush against. (Though sometimes I think it would have been a jolt to climb up onto the tracks and see where my feet took me.)

I guess everyone is subject, to a greater or lesser degree, to his or her environment, no matter if the place be the best of all possible worlds or the worst. In the face of difficult living conditions left of the Loop, Stark adopted a simple philosophy. He said to me one day, "You have to learn how to love it." His philosophy was nowhere better exemplified than in a quote by the filmmaker David Lynch, which he found in *Rolling Stone* and saw fit to write on the wall, quoting it at length. It went like this:

> I love the textures of a factory. I love smoke in the sky, and I love oil in the dirt. And I like wire, and I like broken glass, and I like sweat and pistols. I like a little blood and saliva on concrete. I like cars and exhaust and, I don't know, a million different things. Teeth.

Although I saw much to admire in Stark's philosophy, I felt, being the consummate egomaniac, that it lacked the necessary component of human agency. Put another way, I wasn't satisfied with acceptance, even the loving acceptance exhibited by Stark. But, given my suspicions of knowledge imposed by the mass media, my skepticism of intellectual and moral systems taught or preached in school or church, and my cynicism regarding motives in the political sphere, how to find a code of my own?

As if by design, a method suggested itself one night when I lay on the sofa reading *Gargantua* by Rabelais. In that book there is a long disputation concerning *stichomancy*, the ancient art of divination, which came by way of a random look within the pages of some text. A person who sought guidance would open a book to some prefigured page number, then count down so many lines to the point where his or her prophecy began. Evidently, the *Odyssey*, *Aeneid*, *Bible*, *Koran*, and various other books, both sacred and profane, have been consulted throughout the ages for advice. Upon finishing the passage I decided that, if I had to choose a personal code, one relevant to this particular resident of Outer Bohemia, the advice received through a random process like stichomancy would be most reliable.

Nonbelievers may doubt, perhaps rightfully, the effectiveness of stichomancy, much as they doubt supernatural intervention in human affairs via tarot cards or astrology. They could argue that the process was rigged from the start, for the book chosen would narrow the scope of advice. I, too, was bothered by this possibility. Given the misgivings earlier expressed, religious books like the *Bible* or the *Koran* were out; likewise, books about mythical heroes were also out, because they were written by ancients. I had to find a book pertaining to a late twentieth century American.

I soon convinced myself, however, that fretting too much over what book to choose was a fruitless exercise, one which would devolve into an argument involving the so-called literary canon. Let college professors amuse themselves over such high-toned, but ultimately piddly matters; I had to use a book at hand. So, to begin the process, I picked off my bookshelf an anthology of "Classic American Literature." Originally a textbook from my grad school days, it attempted to present the largest number of authors, contained in the most compact paperback format, printed in the tiniest possible type. Since the book was an anthology, I was satisfied that the range of representative themes would provide a fair and impartial prophecy.

Just to make sure the process was completely random, I watched the Illinois Lottery results on Channel 9 to determine which page and line number to look up in my book. The three-digit Daily Game would provide the page number, the first two numbers from Pick Four the line number. The numbers appearing on the ping pong balls that fateful night were 416 and 3807. Page 416, line 38 put me in the middle of Walt Whitman's *Democratic Vistas*; what follows are the words beginning at line 38:

> Not Nature alone is great in her fields of freedom and the open air, in her storms, the shows of night and day, the mountains, forests, seas—but in the artificial, the work of man too is equally great—in this profusion of teeming

> humanity—in these ingenuities, streets, goods, houses, ships—these hurrying, feverish, electric crowds of men, their complicated business genius, (not least among the geniuses,) and all this mighty, many-threaded wealth and industry concentrated there.

Here was my revelation, a confirmation of longstanding tendencies as well as prophecy: I genuinely *liked* man-made things in my environment, much more so than natural things. I liked how the Merchandise Mart building, like some massive gray butte, dominated the skyline in our view left of the Loop. I liked it better than a real butte, because there are thousands of buttes dotting the land, but only one Merchandise Mart.

Suddenly, it was clear: grandeur lies not in the environment, but resides in the archetypal man, one who can open the mind's eye round enough to encompass the entire horizon and claim it as his own. With these philosophical roots uncovered, I would try my damnedest to farm a hardscrabble Sangamon Street.

# 5 Sickly & Caustic

While living left of the Loop, I worked at Sickly & Caustic, a Chicago law firm on the forty-seventh floor of a downtown skyscraper I called "One Phallocentric Plaza." Every night from five o'clock until midnight I proofread legal documents, losing myself in countless subordinate clauses, acts of God enthusiasms, and paragraphs so long that my workmate and I named weekly winners of the William Faulkner Four-Page-Long Paragraph Award. Any sensible person would laugh if he or she heard the paltry amount of money I earned to take my nightly journey to this mysterious place where the population talked in Legalese—in the halls, up and down elevators, over speaker phones turned up way too loud, and of course in documents worded in the resplendent 18th Century style of the Constitution, but upon reading only contemplating the sale of pigs.

Most of the lawyers were like me according to statistical data the government compiles to describe impersonal attributes like education (graduate or post-graduate), age (21-35), gender (male), race (overwhelmingly white), etc. But when it came to income, that's where the similarity ended and class consciousness began. Somebody once told me that in law firms there are only two possible ranks among attorneys and staff: general and private. However, I sensed that I didn't even rate as high as a private, but rather like the Polish and Hispanic janitorial staff invisibly scrubbing and vacuuming around us all. Only I wasn't dusting off desks or dumping out wastebaskets, I was the guy who cleaned up lawyers' untidy minds.

I have a theory on why this job paid so little, even though I had a college degree and a little bit of graduate school behind me: the work I did, editing legal documents, produced no valuable commodity like steel or peanut butter; that is, no tangible thing came from my efforts. I simply put the finishing touches on what already had been manufactured. Lawyers can be compared to engineers—they design what will be produced, a mortgage or a loan agreement. Then a relatively well-paid word processor uses a computer and printer to generate the document, so it has a physical presence which others find useful. Finally, the document goes to a proofreader, who, like a carwash attendant, wipes off any drips or streaks that remain.

It made no difference that I was good at what I did, and could nightly prove my worth through saving a lawyer's careless ass by making sure verbs agreed with their subjects or that the defendant's name was spelled the same way throughout a document. But since people only pay good money for what they can see or touch, those who live solely by their wits are left out of the transaction. I'm sure this explains why teachers get paid so little, too.

Nevertheless, even with their six-digit salaries and their memberships to the Union League and Downtown Clubs, I felt superior to the lawyers I worked for, because to a person they were incredible dorks. They reminded me of all the kids other fourth, fifth or sixth graders shunned—because they raised their hands too much and answered too many questions; because they smelled vaguely like piss or bacon; or because they dropped every baseball, football and basketball ever thrown to them. No doubt they were nicknamed "Four-Eyes" or "Lizard" or "Beaver," and during recess other kids probably ran away from them for fear of catching "cooties." In short, the lawyers employing me were just like every nerdy kid you ever knew *ever*. The women chewed their nails down to the cuticles; the men sat all wound up at their desks, rocking back and forth, hoping nobody noticed the boners rising up from their laps, as they waited for the teacher to collect the tests they finished first of all the class.

Indeed, my work life seemed just like a continuation of my school life, especially given how the room where I worked was set up: several rows of desks, all facing forward. When these desks were still occupied by first shift proofreaders working overtime, we sat roughly the same distance apart as grade schoolers. At the front of the proofreading room a big, round clock hung on the wall, exactly like the clock in the room where I spent fourth grade. Mounted below the clock was a bulletin board on which my boss Layla stapled helpful hints. Like there are always spaces between the words in the citation "Ill. App. 3d." Replacing the cut-out construction paper letters that spelled out "Meat," "Dairy," "Grains," and "Fruits and Vegetables," we had a chart that showed the proper hyphenation of common legal words, like "pur-su-ant," "Mort-gag-or," "bank-rupt-cy," and "in-ter-rog-a-tor-y." I half expected one day to come into work one night and find illustrations of carved-open frogs or a periodic chart of the elements.

Rounding out the room was a shelf in back where we kept a reference library of dictionaries, citation guides, atlases and telephone books. I often wondered why this shelf couldn't have on it something genuinely cool like a terrarium housing snakes or guinea pigs. We needed such diversions when we were kids to drain off excess energy; I think we need them even more as stressed-out adults. But try to tell that to your boss who believes she pays you to work and not to look at and appreciate dumb little animals.

How did I cope with such an atmosphere, being a man and not a kid? Well, I knew I couldn't beat 'em, so I joined 'em, at least on an individual level, far reduced from that global grab bag into which these lawyers shoved their hands. At the most elemental level, I resorted to my old grade school fireworks. When Layla passed by our door on her way to the women's room, I gave her a minute or two and then started making loud fart sounds between my hands. Sometimes I would load a paper clip into a rubber band sling shot I'd stretched between my first two fingers, then let fly at the clock, enjoying the "Ping!" when I hit its face.

Plus, I continued a habit I picked up in sixth grade study hall of tampering with the bulletin board. Back then I would draw pictures of naked women or peeing men. At Sickly & Caustic, I tacked up subversive cartoons and photographs clipped from radical newspapers and magazines. One time, upon discovering that the firm did litigation for Union Carbide, I tacked up a post-Bhopal disaster Feiffer cartoon which showed a lawyer bragging about his decision to work for the firm representing Union Carbide, and how it earned him "credibility." My grade school teacher would tear off the sheet of construction paper that I had doctored; my surrogate teacher Layla removed my editorial comments in picture form.

More in keeping with the nature of the legal profession's slow sucking away of economic resources, I did things like running off hundreds of copies on the Xerox machine, figuring Sickly & Caustic could afford to contribute to me, a not-for-profit writing enterprise. I also snatched from the storeroom legal pads and Number One pencils, my favorite writing equipment. Some nights I made long distance phone calls, instructing the party at the other end to say he or she didn't know me if Layla ever called to trace the culprit.

From time to time, certain troublesome documents came through our department that required us to proofread still more revisions. Now, with clients like Commonwealth Edison, the electric utility that built underused nuclear plants and then expected rate payers to assume the burden of paying for them, or the Searle Company, which made an IUD device that sent women packing to the hospital with shredded wombs, you'd think one would have to make some sort of accommodation with his conscience in order to fall asleep at night.

To tell the truth, I didn't fret a whole lot over working for a firm that represented such loathsome clients. This wasn't because I didn't have a social conscience like some people might argue, but rather because I did. After all, everybody, even death-mongers like General Electric or Rockwell, should have the right to his day in court. The Constitution considers murderers and rapists innocent until proven guilty; this same protection should likewise extend to corporations. Those who disagree with this viewpoint are the same politically correct people who think that the First Amendment protects only speakers on the liberal side of controversies. There *is* such a thing as being so open-minded that you're closed-minded in your open-mindedness.

Nonetheless, when it came to particularly egregious documents, I simply refused to work on them, leaving them for the day shift. A document that springs to mind was one that tried to justify Northwestern University's move to retain its investments in companies doing business in apartheid-era South Africa. This act of refusal, one which none of my fellow employees knew about, was a powerful thing—a personal brand of civil disobedience. I confess that when confronted with such documents my way was to pass the buck. But to paraphrase thinkers like Lao Tzu and Ralph Waldo Emerson, two men who thought similarly on this subject, I say let the individual reform him or herself first before setting out to reform the rest of an admittedly sick society. To the present day, I always have to remind myself that this view will eventually catch on, and true justice will ultimately be served.

# 6 | The Music In Cans

"Black lung disease?" Stark asked me after I coughed and spat onto the brick street. Rubbing and patting our sweaty bodies with towels, we were walking back to our loft from the Sangamon Track, where we had worked out, if you could call it that, for nearly ten minutes.

"Yeah. You know how exercise brings it up from your lungs," I answered.

Stark laughed, then choked, then coughed and spat himself.

The Sangamon Track stretched along the far side of the train tracks located about two blocks north of our loft. It wasn't any real track, of course; rather, it was a four-block-long slab of concrete set between the Chicago Northwestern triple track mainline on the one side and various spurs which led to the packinghouses on the other side. On weekdays, eighteen-wheelers parked there and were loaded up with meat fork-lifted out of refrigerator cars spotted on the tracks. Since Friday afternoon, however, the neighborhood was devoid of the frantic meat-related commerce normally carried on; being Sunday, this place turned into the Sangamon Track.

Our workout consisted of running a few laps up and down the Track. After a warm-up lap, we timed ourselves with this high-tech stopwatch of Stark's that somehow recorded distance through jiggling while we jogged. The laps we ran were 0.4 miles, a short 600-yard dash. Stark, like usual, had the better time, but this is no surprise, because when I was a junior high schooler I regularly puked running the 600.

"Check that out," Stark said, directing my attention to an individual crawling along the gutter in front of our loft, hand feeling the bricks out in front of him as he crawled.

"He's blind," I said. "Look, he's got one of those white canes and he's wearing sunglasses." From the hand holding his cane, we noted that he dragged a green plastic garbage bag, too. When he came upon a couple dozen beer cans strewn along the curb, probably the same ones Stark and I threw out of our windows the night before when tidying up after band practice, he began to pick them up one by one, crush them between his hands, and drop them into his garbage bag.

"This guy's a priest!" Stark said, seeing his clothes now that he rose up to his knees to perform his can collecting operation. "Look—the black suit, the collar. A priest on the bum on Sangamon Street."

"He's no ordinary priest," I said, looking at his unshaven face, the dusty suit, and, once he stood full up, the worn-out knees to his pants.

Suddenly he spoke.

"Who's there? You're startled. Don't be; I'm not out to hurt anybody. See," he said, tugging at his collar, "I'm one of God's men.

"The name's William Gladfellow, but most folks know me as Blind Reverend Bill. Oh, I know I don't look like a minister, but I assure you I am. Got my Doctor of Divinity at Concordia College in Ft. Wayne, Indiana in 1952. Before that, I earned a B.A. at Indiana University. Unfortunately—or maybe fortunately—God has seen fit for me to experience some changes in my life.

"No. No hedging. I'm one of God's fallen, and what's worse I willingly fell. But I'm slowly working on my redemption, really I am. Nowadays, I live hand to mouth like a bum."

He picked up a couple of cans, crushed them, and tossed them into his bag.

"It's missionary work, really, because I run into good people like you and try to pass on what I've learned. But don't you worry. I'm not going to make you listen to one of those earbeatings like at the mission. It's true—I'm an ordained minister, but I'm no mission stiff.

"This spot here's a gold mine. Of course it's a damn shame when people throw bagfuls of beer cans out their car windows, but at least it means a meager income for me."

Stark and I snickered to ourselves; those were our cans he was picking up.

"I hope you can excuse my picking up these cans while I talk, but I have to work my way back into God's good graces. You understand that don't you?"

We nodded, but of course he couldn't see that.

"Like I said, I haven't always lived like this. I was even pretty good at what I did. After I left the seminary, I got married to woman from a God-fearing family. Her father wanted her to marry a minister, and I seemed a likely candidate. After all, I got a call from a church in Peoria, a downtown one I might add. She was so God-fearing, she insisted on us sleeping in twin beds, so we never had any kids. She didn't believe me when I told her there was an unofficial eleventh commandment which said, 'Thou shalt be fruitful and multiply.'

"She loved me, I guess, though sometimes I doubted it. I'll say one thing for her, though, she was good in her role: The Dutiful Minister's Wife. Why, she *ran* the Peoria Lutheran Wives Collective, and she edited my church's bulletins. But as soon as I went blind and unable to read off my sermons, she divorced me. I caused quite a scandal, let me tell you. This is what I think of romantic love."

He crushed a beer can and threw it into his bag.

"You see, I lost my sight to the demon rum."

He crushed another beer can and tossed it into his bag.

"I'll bet you're wondering how a minister like me, with dozens of sermons published in *Lutheran Bi-Monthly*, became a drunk.

Well, starting in the middle sixties, the make-up of my congregation changed drastically. All the rich people moved to the edge of the city. They stopped coming to my church when Olaf Thornquist, the car dealer, got mugged one Sunday morning after the service.

"Busload after busload of blacks and Mexicans moving north for jobs took over their homes inside of ten years. I guess that life in Peoria turned out to be even harder than in Mississippi or Mexico, because these new arrivals, their spirits broken, often stopped in at the church to receive some counsel. Men who roasted their lungs on the paint line at Caterpillar. Women whose husbands left them with five or six kids to look for work in Chicago or St. Louis, but never came back. Teenagers who thought forming a Youth Group sounded better than joining a street gang. All these people wanted was a little help. But I was so busy trying to rebuild a congregation of the wealthy, I didn't listen and promptly waved them out of my office."

He crushed a beer can and threw it into his bag.

"Wanting an escape, I'd leave my office, say I was making hospital visits, and take a walk. When all the stores moved to the shopping malls at the edge of the city, downtown went completely to pot. In all the storefronts, naked, armless mannequins took the place of mannequins dressed in the latest fashions from Chicago or New York. The only souls that were left downtown after five o'clock were winos and bums. Nothing was keeping anybody else. None of the restaurants stayed open past lunch and all the theaters were boarded shut.

"One afternoon I met a bum called El Loco. Glancing down an alley, I saw him motioning me with his finger to join him. While he handed over his bottle to share sips with me, I told him my troubles. First he laughed at me like the devil was in him, then he sputtered something about wanting to shut off his brain."

He crushed a beer can and threw it into his bag.

"For some mysterious reason, some purpose I came to see was God's alone, I spent more and more time in the streets. Too drunk to go home, I slept many a night on some trash heap, dreaming the dreams of Job. Sometimes when it rained or snowed I'd sleep at the Salvation Army, two bums to a bed. Let me tell you, they were a lot warmer to sleep with than my wife. Then my sight began to fade. I knew why, and so did the president of the local synod, who let me go for neglecting my pulpit. That was when my wife left me, although she was pretty fed up with me for a long time already. You see, when I lost *my* church, I lost *her* church. I just drank more and more, trying to hide it all behind a purple curtain."

He crushed a beer can and tossed it into his bag.

"Since then I've sobered up and taken to following the streets and highways collecting cans for a living. I don't mind at all, really. I may not be able to see, but I sure can *feel* more now than when I had a church. Nothing refreshes me more than crawling in ditches still wet with morning dew. It's like baptism. And the sound . . ."

He crushed the last two cans and dropped them into his bag.

". . . that's music. Do you hear it?"

Stark and I nodded, all we could do.

"Say. What street am I on here?" he asked.

"Sangamon," I said.

"I'm trying to make my way to the Fulton Market."

"Fulton's the next cross street dead ahead," Stark said.

"I've arrived, then. I've been traveling for a good four months now. Some gentlemen I talked to downstate said that the Fulton Market was a place full of food scraps where a bum with my condition could make a decent living. The way they talked, it sounded like the Promised Land."

"We like to think of it that way," said Stark.

"You crawled to Chicago all the way from Peoria?" I asked.

"Yes. Though not in a straight line. Have you gentlemen been on the bum for long?"

"Uh, well, we live in the building here. On the second floor in a loft," I said.

"You're lucky to have a roof over your heads. Most nights I walk all night 'carrying the banner' as my fellow bums say—only I see it as the Banner of Christ."

"You should be careful. A couple of blocks down on Madison Street on Skid Row they'll steal the shoes right off your feet while you're still walking," Stark said.

"That's why I continue to wear my collar. Blind or not, nobody jackrolls a man of God.

"Well, I've got to move along. Beer cans don't come looking for me. Hope my little sermon has raised your spirits some. See you in Heaven."

And so off again he went, crawling and groping his way toward Fulton Street. With that solemn calm you feel when walking out of a church service, Stark and I went upstairs to our loft where we sat down in our chairs and thought hard to ourselves about our broken-down bodies and dissipated souls.

# 7 Dissipation: Definition and Pathology

> Dissipation adds life to your years while it subtracts years from your life.
>
> —Anonymous

Stark and I sat entertaining our old friend Hank Damask in our living room. Fortunately for Hank, he was welcome in our loft, unlike others who dropped by unannounced.

A handful of people we knew, acquaintances or just plain pesky friends who meant well, would stop in periodically. Right when we planted ourselves in front of the TV around kick-off time for a Bears game, we would hear a car horn, somebody yelling up at us from the street, or a rock grazing our windows. Inevitably, the lights would be burning, or the sound on the TV or stereo would be cranked, so we couldn't ignore their beckoning and hope they went away. Always, these friends would drag along some terrified-looking friend of theirs whom we didn't know or, for that matter, didn't care to know.

"Isn't this great?" they would ask, forgetting altogether that they themselves once looked as terrified as their friends. They threw open and shut the big steel door a couple of times to demonstrate its mass and cause ringing in our ears. "This is the room I was telling you about," they said, poking their heads into the Therapy Room and seeing the eight-inch layer of broken glass covering the floor. If we let them stay long enough, visitors might be lucky enough to witness one of us launch a bottle at the wall in there, or maybe they could pitch a couple in themselves.

After taking their friends through the rest of the loft, to the bathroom where the No Pissing sign, a red bar through a penis streaming yellow, draws a laugh, and up the ladder in Stark's room so they could peep into his sleeping area, they would stop at the "Kill Your Pets" graffiti. Usually the poor friend looked at it, then at us, who sat in the living room scowling and shaking our heads, annoyed as lions in a zoo wishing we were racing across the veldt, and, with a nervous frog blocking his throat, asked, "You guys like it here?"

Anyway, at this particular visit by Hank, Stark was not annoyed; he was sitting nicely, not up throwing macaroni and cheese at the walls, off by himself at the windows watching rats running relays across the street, or, a sure sign of pissed-offedness, banging away at the cymbals on either side of his drum set, enjoying the shock waves ripping through his head. Then, slowly and deliberately, he rolled his head back against the wall and rubbed his eyes with the heels of his hands. "Auwgghh! I'm so dissipated," he groaned.

"What's 'dissipated' mean?" asked Hank.

"Well, it's like . . . it's a state of . . . What is it, Stark?" I asked.

"Don't ask me. I'm too dissipated."

"Where's your dictionary?" asked Hank, who always stopped conversations to look up words Stark or I used; although I knew what they meant, I sometimes couldn't define them accurately, usually because I was so dissipated myself. Once, in response to his asking what "prosaic" meant, I said, "Sort of like elephantine." As you'd guess, my explanations hardly ever seemed to satisfy him.

I handed him the dictionary, whereupon Hank paged through the book until he found the word he was searching for.

"'Dis-si-pa-tion,'" he began. "'The act of dissipating.' I guess I'll have to look up 'dissipate.'"

He continued. "'Dissipate: 1. to scatter in various directions; disperse.'"

"That's true," Stark piped up. "Sometimes I feel like those low-lying clouds that I watch roll in and surround the top of the Sears Tower, then split in two and break up."

Hank continued again. "'2. to scatter or spread wastefully; squander. 3. to become scattered or dispersed; be dispelled.'"

"I feel honored to squander the best years of my life here," I announced.

"Back to dissipation," said Hank, laughing. "'2. a wasting by misuse.'"

"That's for sure," I said. "I know I've dissipated a couple million brain cells while living here." I took a big slug of beer. "To think I had a promising career in academia ahead of me."

"C'mon! What's a million more brain cells!" shouted Stark.

"'I've seen the best minds of my generation destroyed by madness, starving hysterical naked,'" quoted Hank. "Here's one," he continued. "'3. amusement or diversion.'"

"Look around you," said Stark. "I *own* this neighborhood. Look across the street sometime. That vacant lot is the Sangamon Picnic Grounds. Every morning I take a jog on the Sangamon track. It's like a damn hotel here, I'm telling you. Call it the Sangamon Arms."

"How about this," said Hank. "'4. dissolute living, especially excessive drinking of liquor; intemperance.'"

"Well, there is a tradition of drinking a lot of beer and smoking a lot of pot here," I said. "There's nothing out the window to look at except guys wheeling around big drums of bones from the packinghouses. You have to do *something* to brace yourself. Hell, we have to drink a lot during winter just to keep warm. That groty old gas stove doesn't heat up all forty-eight hundred square feet, you know."

"Look at this," Stark said, pointing to a message on the wall he wrote a while back. "August 26, 1985, 7:38 p.m. Tick Tick Tick," it said. "I like living here so much that I smoke dope to make the time pass slower. You know about marijuana time? It takes an hour for a pan of water to boil. I figure I'm gonna live to be a hundred and five, marijuana time."

"I see," said Hank. "There's one more definition. '5. *Physics, Mech.* A process in which energy is used or lost without accomplishing useful work, as friction causing a loss of mechanical energy.'"

"That last definition seems the best way to describe life here," I said. "It's a universe by itself with its own physical laws; it's a kind of black hole; it's a vortex that sucks out all the red blood cells from young males between the ages of twenty and thirty."

"It must leave behind the white blood cells, or else I would've been dead from tuberculosis a long time ago," Stark said, kicking up his knees and lying back on the couch.

"You know," I added, "if I didn't live in this loft, I probably would be climbing that corporate ladder right now. But I can't on account of smoking too much. I'm too winded. Hell, I'm not even talking only about business. You don't see me in the chorus of *How to Succeed in Business Without Really Trying*, either."

"You two are dissipators in a dissipating world," Hank said, catching on.

"Maybe we should start a band called The Dissipators," said Stark, rolling over to face the back of the couch. As usual, Stark had the last word concerning dissipation.

# 8 Dissipation Game

One night, when Stark and I felt very dissipated, we hit on the idea of creating a game that would capture the essence of where we lived. We decided that the most characteristic part of living in our loft was how it induced so much dissipation. So we therefore named the new game The Dissipation Game.

Despite feeling truly dissipated, we managed to work together in creating a game board and a set of rules to The Dissipation Game. First we decided on a board. We took some of Stark's construction paper he had left over from covering the various holes he had punched through the flimsy drywall walls that comprised his room, and we cut a square measuring two feet by two feet. Next we marked off around the four edges smaller squares of about two inches by two inches. Finally, taking the configuration of a Monopoly game board as our guide, we penciled in names of locales representative of our Near West Side neighborhood.

I named each location, and Stark doodled a little picture in each square. I decided to make the first side into the "Post-Industrial Urban Apocalypse." For this Stark drew into each of the six squares a rock pile, a drawbridge, an abandoned crane, a broken out windowpane, a mud puddle and a rat. The next side reflected Skid Row. Stark drew a bum suffering from dissipation, a whore with her front teeth blacked out, a wine bottle, an X-rated movie marquee, the front door to a mission, and a black preacher standing on a soapbox. The third side was dedicated to Greek Town. This was easy for Stark. He drew in each of that side's squares a different kind of food: gyros, hamburger, hot dog, shish-ka-bob, baklava, and flaming saganaki with the word "Opah!" written above. I dubbed the last side "Laundry" to somehow depict the Puerto Rican neighborhood to the north of us where we did our laundry. Stark only drew in one thing for this particular side, a box of detergent, because he started to get dissipated again doing all this drawing.

Then we turned our attention to acquiring some playing pieces to go along with the board. We decided that each person would have a different token, a little weird thing also in the spirit of Monopoly. Anything from the loft would work, like cigarette butts, dust balls, paint chips, empty packs of matches, glass shards, whatever. I wanted a cigarette butt to represent me; Stark opted for a shard of glass. I then dug into an old backgammon game I owned and brought out a pair of dice. We felt we had everything to start.

However, we soon tired of simply rolling the dice and traveling around the board. There didn't really seem to be enough conflict to overcome, not enough *fate* entering into the game in order to make it competitive or a challenge. Remembering that Monopoly had a set of "Chance" cards, we decided to incorporate something of the sort to add this missing dimension. What we arrived at was what we called "Setback" cards. The purpose behind the Setback cards was to throw in situations that actually forced you to move your token *backwards*, while rolling the dice moved you forwards.

In this manner, we created a real object to the game, something that brought out a sense of gamesmanship in each of us. The rules we conjured up were simply this: "For Ages 21 to 30. Roll dice in order to advance forward. Setback card taken up with each roll. Move piece backward according to Setback card's instructions. Pass dice to next player for his turn. Game ends when both players have reached age 30. Object: To not be the player who circles the board most moving backwards."

Over the course of a month or two playing The Dissipation Game, we eventually came up with something like sixty Setback cards. The text on some of these cards included:

—Three semis pull up during the night, their fumes wake you up at four a.m. Back 4 sp.

—Have to sweep up a twelve pack's worth of glass after a Bears game. Back 4 sp.

—Cop enters loft by mistake, misses catching you smoke marijuana by five minutes. Back 6 sp.

—Can't find phone bill to mail in when due (it's inside a record sleeve, dumb ass). Back 8 sp.

—You're so dissipated the soup comes out cold and the salad warm. Back 4 sp.

—Toothless whore propositions you, grosses you out. Back 6 sp.

—It seems to take 3 hours for 20 minutes to pass. Back 3 sp.

—Zorba's restaurant is closed for some Greek religious holiday, you can't buy supper. Back 6 sp.

—Box of chicken wings dumped outside your front door, smells to high heaven. Back 12 sp.

—You're down to only one light bulb which you carry from light socket to light socket for 2 days. Back 6 sp.

—Band mates argue for half an hour, singer goes upstairs to sulk for rest of night. Back 12 sp.

—Object accidentally thrown through window, glass everywhere. Back 10 sp.

—Visitor writes dumb things on the wall that you then have to paint over. Back 6 sp.

—You broke your snare drum head. Back 8 sp.

—Six bills come the same day. Back 10 sp.

—Temperatures in the 90s, whole neighborhood smells like rotting flesh. Back 6 sp.

—Acquaintance from five years before drops in unannounced, stays 6 hours. Back 6 sp.

These were the milder forms of setbacks that were possible to those playing The Dissipation Game. To add real interest, we came up with some super-duper setbacks, too, things that happened from time to time which would make a day or even two or three absolutely cataclysmic. These setbacks sent your piece so far back that it would be tough even with a string of double sixes to eventually catch up. Of course, your opponent would also risk picking up one of these super-duper Setback cards, so the winner usually came down to whoever received the least number of super-duper setbacks. Some of these included:

—Temperatures drop to 20 below with 70 below wind chill factor. Back 30 sp.
—Space heater shorts out entire loft, no electricity for 2 days. Back 25 sp.
—While defrosting freezer, roommate stabs hole with screwdriver into freezer wall, all freon escapes, $80 repair bill. Back 30 sp.
—Water pipes freeze, no water for 2 days. Back 30 sp.
—Plastic canopy upstairs designed to catch rainwater leaking through the roof collapses during rainstorm, water floods into loft ruining TV. Back 35 sp.
—Water heater on fritz, no hot water for 3 days. Back 25 sp.
—Broken glass in your foot, doctor removing it costs $60. Back 30 sp.

Stark and I kept track of how many games each of us won. For the most part we were even; I won 236 games, and Stark won 242 games. Like a couple of crotchety old men playing gin, we played the game day in and day out for something like six months, yelling "Goddammit!" at literally thousands of setbacks, although these setbacks sometimes were not necessarily part of the game but *real* setbacks, like, for example, when it cost $80.48 to fix the refrigerator.

We liked the game so much that we wrote to the game maker Milton Bradley and described it to them and asked if they might be interested in marketing it. We explained in our letter that we thought it might be educational, teaching something about industry and culture, sort of like Game of the States, a game both Stark and I enjoyed when we were kids. We added that we realized the game probably wasn't for kids like Game of the States, but we pointed out that there was a big market for adult-oriented games like Pass Out and Strip and Go Naked.

To our great disappointment, Milton Bradley expressed very little enthusiasm for The Dissipation Game. Their letter thanked us for our interest, but claimed that the game simply wasn't *fun*, fun being the first prerequisite for any game they made. We felt good that they took us seriously enough, actually more seriously than we took ourselves, at least to test the market, if that's what they truly did. In any event, we felt paranoid that Milton Bradley would co-opt our idea, and the game would come out within a year, so we registered a copyright with the federal government.

****

Months later, when I was in the process of looking for a stocking cap I misplaced, I ran across The Dissipation Game game board all crinkled up at the bottom of a closet. I remembered how we burned ourselves out playing the game and just gave it up. It reminded me of how, when I was a kid, I would get a toy truck for Christmas or on my birthday, play with it for a whole month straight, then watch how it slowly sank in the toy box under other newer or funner toys, until I finally rediscovered it months later at the bottom of the toy box, unplayed with and forgotten.

# 9 Noh Management

One night late in April, at about three a.m., I woke up with my cheek dug into a wet pillow. If I had lived anywhere else, I would have semi-consciously figured I was drooling in my sleep, flip my pillow over and try to get back to sleep with my mouth shut.

But I lived left of the Loop. For the umpteenth time I woke up in this particular attitude, which caused me to realize the ceiling was leaking again, soaking my bed and me both, and I had better find someplace dry to sleep. Roaring like a rankled bear, I dragged my bed into the living room, a place that in my stupor I knew from experience should be dry. I crawled back underneath the wet covers and, shivering and whimpering, fell back to sleep at about the same rate as the chill-soaked sheets and blankets warmed up to body temperature.

Around dawn, bumping sounds woke me up again. Head raised off my pillow, I saw a mattress come bursting out of Stark's door. This was followed by Stark himself. Both mattress and Stark then flopped onto the floor. "Goddammit!" he shouted, only it was muffled, with his face driven into the mattress. "Fucking woke up in a pool of water," he said, getting up. "Fucking could have drowned in my sleep." I put my glasses on and saw that Stark's hair was ringing wet, as were his Fillmore East tee shirt and his gym trunks.

"I had to evacuate around three," I said.

"Damn mattresses are waterlogged. It'll be a week before they dry out."

"At least it stopped raining."

"The weatherman said there was a zero percent chance of rain. We ought to jam a lightning rod up his ass and tie him to our roof during an electrical storm."

"I guess it doesn't take a weatherman to tell which way the wind blows," I said.

"Guess not."

"Look at this place!" I said, pointing to various puddles on the floor. "This has got to be the worst flood of all time. We ought to withhold rent."

"Screw that! Let's take a bucket of water over to Noh Management and dunk Mr. Mokodam's face in it till they either fix our roof or let him drown."

"They'd call the cops."

"It still might be worth it."

"Let's just not pay rent. I'll write a nice, polite, firm, letter." And so I did, later that morning after Stark left for work. Reviewing my letter after making a couple of minor revisions, I thought it looked pretty good:

210 N. Sangamon
Chicago, IL 60607
April 29, 1986

Dear Noh Management:

We would like to begin this letter by saying that we generally have been satisfied living in your loft at 210 N. Sangamon, and we would like to continue living in it. We of course realize that the place in no way represents high-class living in Chicago, but that is one reason we like it: we have plenty of privacy to pursue our respective artistic careers. And despite some of the hazards of the immediate neighborhood, the building is quite secure. Finally, we like the location, as it is close to our places of employment in the Loop.

We do, however, have some grievances we would like to air in this letter. Of prime importance to us is the ongoing problem of roof leakage. The water pouring into our loft is causing us untold amounts of grief. First and foremost, the water has caused us property damage. Furniture, mattresses, a television set and other personal effects have been stained or rendered unusable. We don't have particularly nice things, but we would prefer to enjoy what we do have in a relatively undamaged condition.

Second, there is a nuisance factor. Always when it rains we have to race around the loft in order to remove things from wet areas. Much of our cooking has been preempted because all of our pots and pans are stationed around the loft to collect the water. The worst nuisance of all is waking up to drops of water striking our foreheads. We have better things to do with our time than dodging raindrops.

Third, there is a safety consideration. The water that reaches our living area is an unhealthy mixture the color of coffee. Also, the loft is precariously wired as it is, so we cannot help but think that the water is creating a further electrical hazard.

In sum, we feel that Noh Management is doing altogether too little to remedy the problem. Indeed, you are compounding the problem. Before your "repairs" on the floor above us, water leaked into one or two places in our loft; after your crude system of plastic tarps collapsed, the dripping has spread to dozens of places. We very much fear that when the early summer rains hit Chicago, we shall again suffer major inconvenience. What we are saying is that solving the problem will require major structural repairs to the roof, not another makeshift system of hammocks strung together. We are asking in this letter that you make such repairs one of your top priorities.

Which suggestion brings us to the unpleasant part of this letter. Being that it is coming up on the first of the month, we originally had planned paying you rent, but now we have decided that we shall withhold rent until we are satisfied that you are doing your utmost to solve this problem. We very much regret having to do this, but the situation has become intolerable. The next rainy weather will be the true test of your attempts. If there are no floods, you shall have your money immediately.

Yours,
I. Spungkdt &
B. Stark

Satisfied that my letter sounded appropriately pathetic, I stuffed it into an envelope and began walking it over to Noh Management's offices near Randolph and Green. While running my errand, I saw on the sidewalk a cardboard carton with a black cloud hovering over it. I figured a step van passed by a moment before and belched out exhaust when downshifting to round the corner. On closer look I discovered, to my horror, that the cloud was comprised of about ten thousand flies revolving top to bottom over the box, which was filled with several dozen raw chicken wings that must have fallen off a truck. I scooted off to Noh Management, trying to put as much distance as I could between that box and me.

While stepping out of an elevator, which had taken me to the top floor of a building full of renovated lofts, I scanned the offices of Noh Management. It was a chore to scan, for the room was double the size of our loft on Sangamon, and it was full of potted plants and trees which camouflaged the occupants of twenty-odd cubicles. Trailblazing through the trees to Mr. Mokodam's desk, I noticed something ominous to our cause: a multitude of Tupperware dishpans catching leaks from the ceiling. Evidently, they had the same problem we had, but they didn't appear nearly so alarmed.

I handed Mr. Mokodam the envelope.

"May rent?" he asked.

"Yeah."

"Okey-dokey," he said, putting the envelope in a drawer to his desk. Imagine his surprise when he opened that letter later on, I thought, feeling pleasantly vengeful.

As I left the building I looked into the bakery on the first floor. For lack of a better description, it was a real yupped-up place, selling croissants, bran muffins and flaky French pastries instead of what suited my simpler tastes: doughnuts and long johns. The bakery was a pioneering effort—the first such yuppie amenity to hit the neighborhood. I personally hoped the business would flop, thus discouraging more yuppie neighbors from flocking to the area, which would spoil a favorite pastime of Stark and me: marching up and down the streets, and declaring in loud voices to the large numbers of people who weren't listening, "This is *our* neighborhood!"

After my contemptuous glare into the bakery, I looked up at the sign above the glass doors. It said in that heavily seriffed, old west script, "Luxury Loft Living in Historic Haymarket Square—From $1,000." I remember thinking that the Haymarket martyrs would be spinning in their graves if they knew that somebody planned to turn the hallowed ground of Haymarket Square into luxury housing and office space and, to boot, were doing so by relying on the historical connotations surrounding the place.

But this impulse seemed destined to prevail. In repetition of an age-old story, wherein speculators moved in and snatched up parcels of land after initial settlement, real estate brokers had discovered that the West Loop was filled with hot properties ready to be cashed in. Loft renovation and its dreaded counterpart, gentrification, was creeping steadily northward from the Eisenhower Expressway. Like squads of soldiers gaining ground through building-by-building assaults, yuppies threatened eventually to displace Stark and me, along with every other civilian who stood in their path.

But I am digressing from my story of our relationship with Noh Management.

I wasn't going to stand for water flooding our loft whenever it stormed; Noh Management would put a new roof on our building or else. A few days after dropping off our letter, I found myself demanding satisfaction from Mr. Mokodam when he phoned to respond. Surprisingly, he understood my outrage and sympathized with our plight. Right off the bat he told me we could subtract a hundred dollars from our rent to help defray the cost of a new TV. Then he promised me full loft renovation—new floors, new windows, a new roof. He said that this was their plan all along, to give us a model loft, and he hinted that the meatpacking houses would close up and move out within a couple of years. In fact, he said, in a month or so, Noh Management meant to move us around the corner temporarily into another building of theirs on Lake Street, while they gutted and sandblasted the shell of our building and renovated the interior. When the work was completed they would move us back in and increase our rent only modestly.

"They started telling me that a couple months after I moved in," said Stark when I informed him of the big news. "It took about eight months till I stopped believing them."

I wasn't a two-year veteran of our loft like Stark, so I truly believed Mr. Mokodam's grand plans, thinking that it would be like heaven, where angels in their stockinged feet slid up and down re-laid floors, beating their wings for speed. But after six months of waiting, my hopes eroded, revealing a substratum of cynicism. From this experience with Mr. Mokodam, I learned the first lesson of dealing with landlords: they always make promises they have no intention of keeping just to string you along. They present you with a relentless set of circumstances that weathers the skull into the wind-swept shape of those rock bridges out west, only it doesn't take millions of years, but six months tops.

****

Some time later, after Noh Management had installed a pretty sturdy set of plastic tarps on both the third and fourth floors, which miraculously held fast during a torrential rain in June, by chance I ran across a cover story on our landlady in a paper called *Inside Downtown Real Estate*, a free weekly describing real estate trends in the Loop and listing properties available for sale or rent. The author of the article drew a portrait of a hyperactive woman pivoting from place to place, idea to idea, and hope to hope, without fixing on any one thing for very long. Unfortunately, as the article made plain, this habit of mind spilled over into her tenants' lives—literally, in the form of brown water washing down their walls.

Admittedly, "The Empress," her nickname according to the article, had come far in her 50 years. Starting out as a second-generation Japanese, whose parents were held captive in a concentration camp in California during World War II, she came east and assembled businesses worth an estimated thirteen million dollars. Noh Management, a company that oversaw seventeen West Loop loft buildings, was only one of several businesses, including a company that stocked vending machines with candy bars and potato chips; Mirabeau's, a fancy French restaurant; and The Crib, a well-reviewed spare rib place.

All of which leads me to the second lesson that applies when dealing with landlords: they always have some job on the side that prevents them from responding to your requests in a timely manner. Instead of improving the creature comforts of her tenants, let alone making their places habitable, The Empress was busy tasting the Chicken Provençal at Mirabeau's or inventing a better system of freeze-drying meat loaf sandwiches for her vending machines. She freely admitted this circumstance in the article:

> My tenants are always calling up to complain about something small, like a leaky bathtub, and they act like it's the most important thing in the world, like the world must stop so their tub gets fixed. Well, it's *not* the most important thing. On any given day, we're renovating three or four properties. I can't tell my workmen to drop everything to fix a leaky bathtub. Angry tenants need to get at the roots of their anger. Maybe their boss yelled at them earlier in the day.

Keep in mind that Stark and I were objecting to wholesale floods, not a leaky tub. Leave it to a landlord to downplay water problems; it allows him or her to sit in a corner office and rake in the dough undisturbed.

At least normal apartment dwellers would have a lease and could petition the city inspectors to enforce their rights under the lease.

But Stark and I didn't have a lease, a fact we were reminded of twice a year when the city sent fire inspectors out to our loft. A day or two before their arrival, Mr. Mokodam would phone and instruct us to leave the loft at the appointed time and lock up our portion. In addition, we were told to hide my motor scooter; the night before the fire inspector's visit found Stark and me dragging my scooter like a recalcitrant yak up the stairs and inside the big sliding steel door. In short, we had to eliminate all evidence that we lived there, because nobody was legally allowed to live on the premises.

The article I read made plain that this shady approach was The Empress's normal mode of business with all the tenants who lived in her buildings around the West Loop. Residents of one of her buildings on Peoria Street found this out the hard way. In response to tenant complaints, the City of Chicago sued Noh Management on their behalf, citing seventy-four pages of code violations. Ironically, the tenants' complaints backfired according to the article—the number one violation concerned people living at an address zoned for light manufacturing purposes. Another round of lawsuits was commenced by the tenants involved, who understandably felt screwed, but they were rendered moot, because, in the coincidence of the century, the building burned to the ground after everyone had been kicked out. The property had a hefty insurance policy tagged to it—over two million dollars—so the police figured it was arson, and The Empress was the obvious suspect. Even after thorough investigations conducted by police detectives and the insurance company involved, neither she nor anyone else was ever arrested for the crime.

Even before the publication of the *Inside Downtown Real Estate* article, Stark appeared to have some vague knowledge about this series of events, so he always talked me out of calling the law on Noh Management, because any complaints would result in eviction, or worse. This brings me to the third and final lesson of dealing with landlords. There is an old adage which says "You can't fight City Hall." My rule is a variation of this old saying and goes like this: "You can't fight landlords with the help of City Hall, especially when you don't have a lease."

So, for the remainder of my stay on Sangamon Street, Stark, Mr. Mokodam and I found ourselves in the position of sitting around the table of an illegal poker game, each one of us holding terrible cards and bluffing constantly, but all three of us aware that any moment somebody could pull the Ace of Spades, the death-by-zoning-law card, from up his sleeve, then call the hand.

# 10 Total Strangers: Part Two

"GODDAMMIT!" Stark yelled at the phone from about six feet away. A split-second later he threw his three-quarters' full bottle of Coke at it, hitting it dead on the dial. "Bullseye," he said, as we watched glass shatter and cola fizz up all over the phone, table and wall. Knocked clear off, the handset started to honk faintly, an electronic goose letting us know we should hang it back up again.

"Who were you on the phone with?" I asked, fearing it might be his sister calling with bad news about some dead relative, while at the same time barely concealing my desire to laugh my ass off at what happened to the phone.

"Rudy the Roach," he said. "They're coming over tonight for band practice. I sure as hell don't feel like dealing with them. Why can't they skip a Sunday once in a while and leave us alone for a night?"

"You still pissed they kicked you out of the band?"

"No, not really. And I'd say it was more mutual than them kicking me out. I'd say I quit because none of them could get their act together enough to take it anywhere, let alone on the road."

"'You can't quit me, I fire,'" I said, quoting Rob Petrie on the old *Dick Van Dyke* show.

"Why did you say that?" he asked.

"Rudy called today wanting to know if Wanda left her sunglasses here last Thursday night. I said I hadn't seen them.

He tried to talk me into looking around the loft for them and calling him back. I didn't want to deal with him, so I said again, 'I haven't seen them.' I think the way I leaned on the word 'haven't' got my point across, because then he changed the subject and asked how you took getting fired from the band."

"That asshole. Now I *really* don't want them to come over."

"What did you say to him on the phone? You sounded pretty dissipated."

"I tried to sound that way, like I was sick or something. But I was civil, at least till I hung up and threw my Coke at the phone." He looked inside the refrigerator. "That was the last Coke, too, goddammit!" he added, slamming shut the refrigerator door, which bounced wide open, then slowly shut again for good.

"Why did you agree to let them keep coming over for band practice if you quit?"

"It's only temporary till they find more rehearsal space. He talked me into it, and I promised. Thing is, you know how they take over when they're over here. It's like a bad horror movie called *Invasion of The Strangers*."

"I haven't been here when they were here since you quit. How long's it been?"

"A couple of weeks, since about the beginning of February. Rudy's even more obnoxious now that I've quit, because not only is he coming over to rehearse, but he thinks he's paying me a social call, too. Some nights he drops by an hour, hour and a half, before he's supposed to."

"Who do they have playing drums?"

"This guy. Rudy said he used to play with a guy who played with some guy who used to play for Nick Lowe. Or some shit like that. I guess he's pretty good. His time's better than mine, I'll say that for him, but that's only because he's been playing for fifteen years, and I've only played for four."

"You must really dread them coming over."

"Yeah," he sighed. All the adrenaline juicing up Stark after throwing his Coke at the phone seemed to be exhaled with this one sigh. His earlier pacing around the loft ended, and he plopped down on the couch, utterly dissipated.

Maybe some of those adrenaline molecules which filled the loft after Stark's heavy sigh found their way into my lungs and then went to my head, for, a minute or two later, I said, "We ought to invite a bunch of people over ourselves. Like Hank Damask and Rick O'Shea. It'll be like our gang won't let their gang take over the loft."

This suggestion woke Stark right up. "Great idea. I'll make the calls, if the phone still works." He walked over to the phone, dialed, and when he heard it starting to ring, he gave me a thumbs-up sign. Only he held the handset a good six inches from his head.

"Can you hear holding it away from your ear like that?"

"I'll have to. I'm sure I don't have to tell you how sticky the phone is right now."

****

Hank Damask was the first to arrive. We wasted no time in firing up a bong and passing it around. On Hank's second hit he began to cough violently. After thumping himself in the chest with his fist a couple of times, he appeared to recover. I came back to the living room from the kitchen where I fetched Hank some water in a bowl because we only owned three drinking glasses and none was clean. "Old smoke," Stark was saying, shaking his head like a fatalistic country doctor who had seen plenty of this kind of thing before.

"Old smoke?" asked Hank.

"Yeah, this," Stark said, snapping the plastic lid off the top of the bong's water chamber, an act which revealed a cocklebur of brown smoke rotating slowly above the water line. "After every hit, you have to take the top off and blow it out." He blew gently at the smoke, dispersing it. "Old smoke is the harsh residue left in the bong because there's no carburetor. It only takes ten seconds for sweet smoke to turn into old smoke. I've timed it."

"I'll certainly try to be more careful," Hank said. After saying this, he cocked his head and pricked up his ears.

I, too, had to cock my head to hear what he was hearing, and when I did, I recognized the sounds right away: footsteps upstairs traveling from the northwest corner of the loft to the southeast corner. "I think we have a bum upstairs," I said to Stark.

Stark bolted to the big steel sliding door and yelled up the stairway in his snarliest voice, "HEY YOU! GET THE FUCK OUTTA HERE!" Then he quickly flung the door shut and threaded the padlock through the latch.

We periodically had unwelcome visitors to our building. Our part of the loft was on the second floor and sealed off by the big steel sliding door, but there were two vacant floors above us that just about anybody could reach if the street door downstairs was left open, which it often was by Joe, the guy who owned the used printing equipment business on the first floor. We figured we really had nothing directly to fear from such people; more than anything, we felt sorry for them, and we wished we were in the position to do something, anything, to help them out. We also knew, however, that if it were cold enough and somebody started a fire, it would quickly spread down to our floor, a fear confirmed one day when we watched a loft building exactly like ours a few blocks west on Ada Street be completely engulfed in flames inside of ten minutes.

Perhaps we acted awfully paranoid, I don't know. Regardless, despite our inclinations to live and let live, we yelled at strangers upstairs to get the fuck out of our loft, which, luckily, they promptly did.

"You're playing with fire," Hank warned Stark.

"They'll play with fire if I don't play with fire first," said Stark.

Hank said something else, too, but I can't remember what it was; I was too busy to listen because I kept listening for the downstairs door to open and slam, but sixty or ninety seconds later, I still hadn't heard those two sounds yet. Then metallic whumping sounds erupted from the big steel sliding door.

"Holy shit!" Stark and Hank said simultaneously. "Who the fuck is it?" Stark yelled, although there was a nervous twitter in Stark's voice on the word "fuck." There was no reply.

Somebody had to do it, so I went over and opened the door. "Hey! Is that any kind of way to greet an invitee?" said Rick O'Shea, who slipped sideways through the one foot-wide space I opened for him; I wouldn't open the door any further, because, with the bulb on the landing burned out, I couldn't truly tell who was at the door until he came full into the loft, and he began to shake my hand, asking, "How's it going?"

"Rick O'Shea" wasn't our friend's real name. Stark and I called him that anyway, even though back in college, where we all originally met, I knew him as "Tony Demencia," which I don't think was his real name, either. Having lived out west for a year, I had lost touch of Rick and Rick's purpose for changing his name; Stark once explained to me that he understood Rick owed the phone, gas, electric and cable companies money, so he kept changing his name and moving to avoid "sheriff's police and summons servers and shit." Whatever his name, since dropping out of school he managed to stay out of jail, and he made an okay living stuffing envelopes for ten hours a day in between musical gigs.

"We thought you were an pyromaniac," said Hank.

"I shinnied up the drain pipe on the alley side of the building," Rick explained. "About twenty feet up I had to jump about three feet to my left to catch the fire escape. The windows were sealed on the second and third floors, so I had to come down from the fourth floor."

"I would've come down to let you in," Stark said.

"No challenge. You'll never catch a buzz that way." He pulled a pint bottle of rum out of his coat pocket and took a healthy swig.

"I brought that too," said Hank, pointing to his own pint bottle of rum and holding up his glass to show the brown liquor it contained. The coincidence of these two drinking the same drink really was no coincidence at all; a couple of years back both Rick and Hank played together in an all-white reggae band with the same name as their rum. This band toured the big cities and college towns of the Midwest for about two years, going as far west as Kansas City, as far north as Minneapolis, as far south as Nashville(!), and as far east as Columbus, Ohio.

"Wait till you see what else I brought," said Rick. "A four track. It's out in my trunk. We can record the band."

The four of us burst into laughter.

"That'll really put them on the spot," said Stark. "The more disruptive stuff the better." When the laughter died down a good eight or ten minutes later, Rick went downstairs to bring the tape deck up from his car.

"Not to change the subject, but have you ever smelled Wanda, Hank?" I asked. Stark laughed.

"No, I don't generally make a habit of smelling people . . ."

"Me neither, but with her it's so in your face, you can't help it. Stark thinks she smells like sushi; I say she smells like beaver pelts."

"I'll have to remember to keep downwind from her," said Hank. "Which way's the draft in here coming from?"

"You're left of the Loop. It comes from whichever direction you're facing," said Stark, in a neat variation on the folk wisdom regarding Chicago and the wind.

Rick returned wrestling with a bulky machine that evidently was the four track. It looked to me like a regular old reel-to-reel tape recorder built onto a mixing board. Somehow, I was expecting something more. Anyway, behind Rick there were Rudy the Roach and Wanda, along with still another new guy, one of a whole string of characters stretching through the band years, always somebody new and different, and never back a second time. Stark quickly pocketed the bag of marijuana.

"Everybody!" Rudy called. "This is Clay, our new drummer. That's Ish, you know Stark, that's Rick and that's Hank."

"How often do you yank, Hank?" asked Clay.

"What kind of question is that?" asked the offended Hank, but Clay didn't answer; rather, he bypassed the living room altogether and progressed to Stark's drum set, where he started to examine it, ignoring everyone.

"Clay's a real thoroughbred," said Rudy. "Do you know about his old band, The Rip Roarings? They were a Rockabilly band out of Evanston. They went major label on their second album, but then their guitarist quit the band to do studio work for Nick Lowe, and the band broke up."

"And now he's playing with The Strangers," said Stark. He lifted his hand and showed us his thumb and forefinger, which were spread about an inch apart. "To think he's this close to playing with Nick Lowe."

"Have to use your kit tonight, Stark," shouted Clay from over in the band area. "Mine's still en route from Lake Geneva from a recording gig I had up there last week. Think they'll hold up?"

"They better," Stark said, and then he went into his bedroom. He motioned me to follow, which I did. I got it; he wanted to continue smoking dope with Rick, Hank and me, but he didn't want to share any with the band.

After a few hits, I returned to the living room. In my absence the rest of the band had shown up—Danny, their bass player, and a guy everyone called Happy Jack, a lead guitarist who had stuck it out for nearly two months, a new record for a band that changed lead guitarists every other week. I bent over to whisper in Rick's ear that he should pay a visit to Stark's room. He tapped Hank on the shoulder, and both of them disappeared behind Stark's bedroom door, leaving me alone with the band. Everybody who remained looked at me expectantly.

"You got any dope?" Clay asked finally.

"Nope, sorry, we're out," I said.

"What about your friends? What about Yank?"

"I think they're out, too."

"What about some toot? That's what they're doing in the other room, right? They're doing toot," he said.

"If they are, then they're not including me. But that's okay, because I don't much care for the stuff."

"You don't like toot? *Everybody* likes toot . . ."

"Imagine that! Stark and Spungkdt out of pot. Guess we'll have to play straight for a change," said a sarcastic Rudy, thankfully deflecting Clay's interrogation. It was obvious he didn't believe me either; I was afraid he would start his own line of questioning, one that probably would trap me in my lie if pursued relentlessly enough, but, fortunately, he led the band over to the band area, where they began to unpack their instruments and tune up. Everybody, that is, except Clay, who walked over to Stark's door and began pounding on it, saying, "You guys are doing toot in there. I know you are."

Once they heard Clay thump his bass drum a couple times, which signaled to them that he had settled behind his drums and that it was safe to come out of Stark's room, Stark, Rick and Hank rejoined the rest of us scattered around the loft. Stark and Hank sat with me in the living room area; over in the band area, Rick started his tape deck rewinding, and he began plugging cables from the microphones and amps into the back of it. The loft seemed like a boxing ring to me the way our gang sat in one corner, and the band staked out their corner opposite.

After a couple of dirty looks at Rick and Rudy, who were busily debating where Rick should place the microphones, Wanda announced that she was sick and tired of standing around, and she came to sit by Stark, Hank and me in the living room. Even though it was late February and pretty cold outside (and inside the loft, too, for that matter), she was skimpily dressed, wearing a pale green sleeveless t-shirt that, to be honest, clashed with her white china doll skin, a leather mini skirt, pumps and no panty hose. Although it appeared freshly washed, her tee shirt nonetheless had what looked like bleach spots down the front of it. When she raised her hand to her face, to scrape away a make-up fleck with her pinky nail, I noticed that she didn't shave under her arms. Besides no panty hose, I guessed that she wasn't wearing a bra either. In my usual spot, sitting behind the desk, and with her positioning—sitting sideways directly in front of me on the sofa—I had a nearly perfect sight line through her tee shirt's left arm opening and into her bosom. Determining that she indeed was not wearing a bra gave me something of a thrill, admittedly a cheap thrill, but a thrill nonetheless.

Not exactly knowing what to say to Wanda, and seeing neither Stark nor Hank saying anything, I finally said something safely inoffensive: "You look nice tonight."

"You think so, really?" she asked, standing up to primp for the three of us. Then she patted the insides of her thighs and said, "My thighs are getting too fat, I think. What do you guys think?"

"No, no, no, they're perfect," we all chimed at once. I don't know about Stark, who preferred a more classically pretty look, or Hank, who liked boys, but I, who found her earthiness appealing, truly believed her legs were perfect.

Then I really put my foot in it. "You smell like leather tonight."

Hank instantly broke into uncontrollable laughter. And then Stark joined in. I, too, was infected with laughter, but I tried to squelch it, because I saw that Wanda was looking dumbfoundedly at us. Then a hurt and insulted look crossed her face, and tears came to her eyes. She rose and abruptly walked out the big steel sliding door. We heard her climbing the stairs, and then we heard her wandering around upstairs until her footsteps came to a halt somewhere in the back corner of the third floor.

"Now look what you guys have done," I said to Stark and Hank. "You hurt her feelings."

"It was you," Hank said. "I lost it because you were talking about how she smelled earlier. And then you said that. I couldn't help it."

"That was the most important disruption of the night you made there—making them rehearse without Wanda," said Stark.

"I didn't mean to . . ."

"We're ready now," Rudy called over from the band area. Then he asked, "Where's Wanda?" Getting no reply and looking around for the reason why, it dawned on him that she must have left the loft.

"I think she went upstairs to sulk," said Stark.

"Great. We're getting some free recording time, and she skips out."

"It'll be no problem," said Rick. "We can dub her parts in later."

"What did you do to her?" Rudy asked.

"Nothing," I lied. I felt bad about my complicity in her hasty exit, but I thought twice about confessing, so I decided to cover up. "You know women," I continued. "They're a strange species. They're even stranger than duck-billed platypuses."

"You've got that right," said Rudy.

Then, tape rolling, the band kicked into the first song of their rehearsal. The now-familiar strains of Rudy's song, "Pepsi Cola in Petrograd," a song decrying the Soviet sellout to hollow Western consumerism, filtered through the loft.

Meantime, except for Rick, who still was fiddling with the four track, our corner began exploring ideas for further disrupting the band. Something loud was out, because their P.A. system could easily drown out practically any noise we made short of explosion. Something too obviously malevolent, like unplugging their amps or throwing Stark's old cracked cymbals at their feet, was also out. "Too much danger of starting a fight," I said.

"I know!" Stark blurted out. "Let's play Reverse." He ran into his room to get the three rubber balls needed to play the game.

"Leave it to a sociopath like Stark," Hank said to me as we took our positions on the Reverse Court, the whole empty middle part of the loft we called the Sangamon Gym.

"Looks like we have some dancers," Rudy called out to the rest of the band.

Stark took a while to find the balls, but before too long he threw open the door and tossed a ball to each of Hank and me, keeping one for himself.

Three players were needed to play the game Reverse, and you needed one rubber ball per player. I picked up the balls we used one afternoon on my way to work on the el, buying them from a guy who walked up and down the aisle of the train peddling lots of oddball things he carried in clear plastic bags, like disposable lighters, tube socks, and pink, Korean-made teddy bears. In addition, he had bundles of things tied to his back, like umbrellas and White Sox pennants. He offered me a good deal on rubber balls painted in fluorescent colors and all different designs, so I bought three from him for something like a buck. Reverse was the game we invented to make use of the balls after we discovered that a simple game of catch was a bore.

The object of the game simply was to pass the balls around a circle made by the players, each player throwing his ball to the player on the right and immediately turning around to catch a ball thrown from the player on the left. Basically, the challenge was to throw and catch simultaneously, without overthrowing the player ahead of you, or missing a catch from the other player throwing from behind you.

Stark and I were pretty skilled at the game; we had considerable practice throwing two balls among ourselves in a back and forth loop. However, Hank wasn't so hot at the game—he threw the ball underhand, so it often arched over my head, and he missed a bunch of tough but catchable knee-high tosses from Stark. Nevertheless, to give him all the credit he deserved, he grew a little more proficient the more times the balls went around the circle. At one point we had a good rhythm going, one that fell perfectly in sync with a song the band was playing.

The song, "Bludgeoning Love," was a ballad in four; as the song played, we tossed the balls to one another exactly on the beat. In one spot of the song, we went a whole twenty-four bars without flubbing up, meaning we successfully threw the ball to each other a total of 72 times.

Although I saw out of the corner of my eye that Rudy and the rest of the band seemed to be showing off to us, and especially to Stark, they soon realized, as indicated by the disappearance of all the guitar poses and rock and roll faces, that we were ignoring their performance. Indeed, rather than our gang being a captive audience of their rehearsal, our roles had, well, *reversed*—in between notes their gang became distracted watching our gang play Reverse.

"Whoa! Everybody! Hold it!" said Rick about midway through the song "Super Mental Masturbators."

Rudy waved at the band to halt the song. "What is it?" he asked.

"In between songs I forgot to let the pause button up, so none of this song has recorded. I'm sorry. I was watching those guys play catch, and I forgot."

"Ooops," Stark said.

"No problem," said Rudy, although he betrayed this sentiment through an exasperated sigh that followed.

"Tape's rolling now," said Rick, and the band played the song from the top.

One other rule in Reverse I so far have neglected to mention, the rule from which the game got its name, was that anytime during the game a player was allowed to call out the word "Reverse." At this cue, the players had to throw the ball back the way it came, in effect reversing the clockwise motion of the balls to counter-clockwise. As you can expect, this moment precipitated all kinds of chaos, as the players snapped out of the lull induced by going all one direction. What usually resulted were dropped balls, or worse, overthrown balls that disappeared under furniture. With practice, however, these reversals in direction could be handled with a minimum of jerky or awkward moves.

"REVERSE!" Stark called out. The direction we were going had me throwing to Stark and catching balls thrown from Hank. Experiencing the same kind of heads-up chaos which ensues during an interception in football or a turnover in basketball, we reversed direction. I threw the ball Hank just threw me back to Hank. Stark threw his ball at Hank, too. Problem was, Stark was supposed to throw his ball to me. Instead of catching at least one ball, which is what Stark or I would do, Hank dodged the two balls thrown at him. One deflected off him and bounced harmlessly between Rudy and Danny; the other shot straight by Hank and struck Happy Jack's guitar strings, making that Barranginging! sound of unfingered strings sustaining amongst the amp and room for a while and then gradually fading.

The band stopped.

"Can't you guys be more careful? We're recording god fucking dammit!" Rudy yelled at the three of us.

"Yeah!" Rick said. He made an exaggerated display of punching the stop button on his tape player. (A few days later, Rick came by with copies of the tape, one for Rudy to pick up and one for Stark and me. On Rudy's tape, he erased the song disrupted by the stray ball, but on our tape, he kept it. For the rest of the time Stark and I were roommates, one of us occasionally would put this tape in our deck. The "Barranging" sound butting into the song, followed by Rudy's admonishment, never failed to produce a good ten minutes of hooting and howling.)

"Sorry about the out-of-bounds ball," Stark said, crawling underfoot of the band to find and retrieve the two guilty balls.

"We can record it again," said Rick.

"Sorry about all these distractions," Rudy said, directing his apology to Clay. "It's just like at CBGB's when I was running sound on Jim Carroll's demo tape for Warner Brothers. There were all these drunk, underage kids reaching up and grabbing his legs while he was trying to sing."

"We've done our duty, Rudy. How about a break?" Clay responded.

Rudy, Danny and Jack unstrapped their guitars and went to sit in the living room. Our gang decided we needed a break, too, so we joined them. Before coming to the living room, Rick rewound the tape, and started to play it for everybody. To tell the truth, even with the distractions going on, Rick did an admirable job of recording the band, which, I have to say, sounded better than I remembered. The tape still needed mixing, but he had good stuff to work with—Clay was a more solid drummer than Stark, and Rudy's rhythm guitar had a less muddy tone than usual. Still, Wanda's voice was sorely missed; I remember thinking that the band's overall improvement possibly stemmed from her absence, but I hoped the pace of her improvement kept up with the rest of the band's.

As if to put her to the test, Wanda came back down to the loft from upstairs. "Rudy! I found my sunglasses upstairs. I must have left them up there during break last week."

"You mean during your pouting session last week," I heard Stark say under his breath.

Rudy greeted her at the door and put his arm around her. Walking her back out the door again, he began to whisper whatever soothing words he always said in order to calm her down and motivate her.

A couple of minutes later, they returned, and Wanda said, "I'm sorry everybody for my bratty behavior. I'm ready to record now." Rick stationed himself behind his four track and began to slide switches and turn knobs preparing it to lay down Wanda's vocals.

"Here, put these on," Rick said, handing Wanda a pair of headphones. "The instrumentals will be piped in through the headphones, and you'll sing along into this microphone right here." He tilted the microphone so it pointed just beneath her lips.

After a deep breath, Wanda began to sing the first song, "Pepsi Cola in Petrograd." Surprisingly, given his habit of swarming all over Wanda and posing her when she sang, Rudy allowed Rick to take over, and he sat down with the rest of us in the living room. You could tell by his firm-clenched fists thumping to the beat on the love seat's arm that he somehow was willing her to sing her best. All the rest of us guys in the loft fixed our eyes and ears on her, responding to her singing in each of our varyingly critical ways. The first thing I personally realized, something glaringly apparent with her alone and no band accompanying her that I could hear, was that she still had that disturbing problem with intonation. In addition, she was stiff—hands moving tentatively, if at all, no bouncing at the knees—probably from concentrating so hard that something pinched.

In her favor, I was glad to see that she had abandoned that falsified, yap hound sound which may have been trendy and cute, but which was limited, and instead had adopted, against Rudy's earlier advice, a husky, more natural quality. Another plus: she had developed more breath support, and therefore more volume, since the last time I heard her sing. It was an essential skill for her to learn, for her natural voice was in a low register for a woman, a range almost lower than Rudy the Roach's twirpy, high tenor range. The deep range, coupled with the husky quality, created a sexually potent mix, one that overrode most of her musical handicaps. Overall, I'd say she sounded more aggressive and less wishy-washy than when I first heard her sing the previous spring.

"Don't worry," Rick said to Rudy, breaking our silence. "I can put a little reverb in and help her out with her pitch."

"Pitch? She sounds like Nico right now. Don't change a thing."

"She's flat in spots. A little reverb will wash out the flat spots, make her sound real good."

"You don't think she sounds good? This time last year she was a coke fiend. Now look at her."

"I'm not cutting her down," said Rick. "I'm coming from a producer's point of view. I want to make her sound better on tape than she does in real life."

"Then you must not know what a natural talent Wanda is. She doesn't need any electronics watering her down. Having somebody with her combination of talent and looks fronting the band, we'll go national inside of three years. Stark's a rock and roller. He knows the formula. Tell him, Stark."

"I think she's pretty one-dimensional," Stark replied.

"Listen. I taught Wanda everything she knows about rock and roll. I'm her mentor. If you call *her* one-dimensional, then you call *me* one-dimensional." He stopped talking momentarily and looked over at Wanda to check if she was hearing any of our conversation, which was heating up too much for me, but which, I'm sure, made Stark feel very warm and self-satisfied given his recent history with the band.

Seemingly oblivious, Wanda was bobbing her head and singing some lines from the band's cover version of the classic Petula Clark number "Downtown."

"Listen to that, you guys," Rudy said. "That's pure soul. Pitch is irrelevant to somebody like her. It's what you prefer: chops or raw talent. You evidently want chops. If it were me, I'd pick talent."

Rudy was correct in that, I remember thinking—pitch *was* irrelevant to Wanda. Still and all, even with her tantrums and her intonation problems, I had to agree that Wanda possessed some sort of indefinable magnetism which Rudy was working to extract; but whether for love or his own commercial gain, it wasn't yet clear to me.

"What do you guys think?" Rudy asked, looking at Danny and Jack.

For most of the evening, neither Danny nor Jack said much of anything during our match of wits between their gang and our gang; rather than risk getting involved, they chose to look down at the floor embarrassedly. They continued this practice in response to Rudy's goading.

"How about you, Clay? You're a professional musician." He lit up his last cigarette. "You should know better than these pretend rock critics." He crumpled up the empty cigarette pack and angrily threw it down on the floor.

Stark jerked forward in his chair, ready to rise up. I knew why: Rudy had thrown the gauntlet down, so to speak, in an affront to Stark's knowledge of rock and roll and his taste in music generally. I doubt if Stark would have slugged Rudy—Stark always took out his anger on inanimate objects like bottles or the telephone and not on people—but I could tell he was plenty riled and about to say or do something ugly.

Then Clay cut the tension in the air with his big, thick, broadsword tongue. He said, "Well, it's just about dark, Stark. If you've got any toot stashed away, then you better bring it out now. We start any later, and we're going to be up till six a.m. arguing about this shit."

Everybody, our gang and their gang included, exploded with laughter. Then Rudy shooshed us down really quick, because he didn't want Wanda to get all self-conscious and think we were laughing at her. "'Bludgeoning Love' is coming up next on the tape," he said. "I better go over and coach her through it."

Still snickering and shaking his head at Clay's goofy suggestion, he stood beside Wanda as she finished up singing "Downtown."

"You're smirking at me again," Wanda complained to Rudy in the space between songs. Then she attempted to pull the headphones off, struggling with them like she was fighting with a crab clamped onto her head.

When she finally succeeded in getting the headphones off, she threw them at Rudy, who made a good shoulder catch and said, "Honest Wanda, I wasn't smirking at you. It was Clay. He said something funny. Not about your singing, something else totally. You were doing a crackerjack job . . ."

But in the meantime, she had turned her back on him and walked out the big steel sliding door without saying another word. Rudy went over to the window. After a minute or so of looking out and watching her, he turned to us and said, "I thought she was going to sit on the curb and pout like she always does. But she walked up to Lake Street and headed left towards Halsted."

"She'll be fine. I bet she goes down by Barney's Market Club and catches a cab. She'll probably be waiting at home for you," I said.

"I hope so. I hope she doesn't get lost on the way home. I'd kill myself if she ended up dead in a dumpster inside Cabrini-Green."

"I doubt if she'd end up there," said Danny. "She's not black and on welfare. In the projects they only go for their own kind."

"I'm worried, though. She's such a geographical handicap. She can't tell the difference between 'Ashland' and 'Addison.'"

"Do you think she'd find someplace if you told her it was on the corner of Ashland and Addison?" asked Rick, more or less rhetorically.

Positively flustered, Rudy waved off what he considered a stupid question. "This is serious! She's never up and left by herself before."

"She's definitely got ants in her pants," Hank observed.

"You would, too, if you had her star quality," Rudy snapped.

"If I had her star quality I'd probably be a female impersonator singing torch songs for a living. I certainly wouldn't be wasting my time hanging around with you guys," said Hank.

Evidently, all of us were wasting Stark's time; he was prowling around the Sangamon Gym for something to do. I thought he might pick up one of Rick or Hank's empty rum bottles and throw it at the wall in the therapy room, something I know would undissipate him. Instead, he poked his hand into a garbage bag and pulled out an empty, gallon-sized, plastic milk jug. He dug further and found the cap, which he screwed back onto the jug. Then he picked up the table leg he kept from his early days on Sangamon, when he was naive enough to believe he needed a weapon of some sort for protection. Finally, standing in a batter's stance, he pitched the milk jug up into the air and swung at it with the table leg, hitting a pop foul, which shot behind him and crashed through one of our windows. "Batter Up!" he said, accompanied by sounds of glass breaking on the sidewalk below.

"Jesus Christ!" said Jack. "Aren't you gonna have to pay for that?"

"Naw," said Stark. "We just call up the management company and tell them some asshole threw a rock through our window and could they please send somebody out to fix it. How many times have we done that now, Ish?"

"I don't know. Three or four."

Rudy all the while sat hunched over the desk, rubbing his eyes and pinching the bridge of his nose; he didn't appear to notice what happened to our window. He wearily stood up and said, "I'm going to try to catch up with Wanda." Then he pulled me aside. "Say, Ish. I'm really stressed out. I know you guys don't have any pot, but if you could give me, like, five or ten cigarettes, I'd be in your debt forever."

"I can give you maybe one or two," I said. "But I'm almost out myself." I tore the gold foil off the top of my last pack of Benson and Hedges, and showed him that I only had four cigarettes left.

"That's okay. I'll scrape some tobacco together and roll one." He went to each and every ashtray in the loft, collected all the butts that he and I had left behind, then proceeded to tear them open and empty their contents onto the desk. He pulled out some rolling papers, and with the tobacco he gathered he rolled a cigarette not much thicker than a toothpick. Lighting up, he announced, "I'm outta here. Yo! Rick! I'll call you later this week about what we got down on tape."

Rick only nodded his assent, for he was engaged in a game of 500 which the rest of the guys who remained in the loft were in the process of playing. Stark had gone downstairs to retrieve the milk jug he walloped through the window, and he was batting grounders and flies to everybody standing in a semi-circle around him. When Clay scooped up a one-hopper hit his way, thereby reaching 250, he insisted that Stark had been at bat for long enough, that at the rate they were going nobody else would get a turn, and that since he had high score, he should bat next. Everyone agreed with his reasoning, so the seven of us, playing 250 together, took turns batting and chasing the milk jug flip-flopping around the loft until about midnight. Fortunately, no more windows were broken, but we did lose a coffee mug and two light bulbs in the course of our game.

# 11 Hog Butcher for the World

Standing at the window one day, daydreaming, Stark spotted two flesh-colored lumps on the sidewalk across the street. "Hey, I wonder what this is?" he asked, motioning me over to the window.

I looked out and he looked out, both of us myopic and wearing glasses, squinting our hardest, craning our necks to make out the identity of the lumps, or could they be two flat stones?

"They're pigs' heads!" I blurted out, horrified, but at the same time curious. "Let's go over and look at em up close!" I said. Stark didn't even answer; he broke into a dead run out the door, down the stairs and onto Sangamon Street.

When I caught up with him in the middle of the street on the way over to the pigs' heads, he just looked at me and said "Yeah," and then he laughed dementedly, his eyes now recognizing their forms.

We crept slowly toward the pigs' heads like poaching dogs do, steering just to the right, sniffing out the situation, not quite sure yet if the rabbit or quail or whatever will up and run away.

The pigs' heads appeared freshly severed: quite motionless and dead. Thankfully, their eyes were shut, and no more blood dripped from under the sawtoothed skin that used to be their necks.

"These are cool. They're cool as hell. They're the coolest thing I've ever seen on Sangamon," Stark said.

"What should we do with em?" I asked.

"Watch em *decay*, man! It'll be cool, you watch."

So we left the pigs' heads there, and we monitored their progress daily from up at the window or when we walked someplace like the L stop on Halsted.

We noticed very little change the first few days aside from dust and exhaust settling on them, peppering them. A week later, Stark noticed that one had moved about a foot closer to the curb. We guessed either a drunk waddling down the street kicked it, or maybe a rat gave up trying to drag it away.

Soon thereafter, my friend Stevo, who lived some sixty miles west of Chicago, visited us on Sangamon. Naturally, we showed him the pigs' heads, the newest addition to the Sangamon Street show and tell repertoire. We knew he'd like them, because he was a farm boy by upbringing, and a monster movie watcher by inclination. Stark and I noticed that the pigs' heads had darkened since the last time we checked them; they almost seemed to draw their color from within now—footprints marching beneath the skin instead of on top.

"I'm gonna spraypaint one!" Stevo declared.

"YEAH!" Stark and I simultaneously cheered, throwing up our hands and shaking our fists at the sky.

Stevo came back down from our loft carrying two cans of spraypaint we used to write or draw on the wall. Damn him if he didn't just step right up to one of the pigs' heads and then let fly with the spraypaint. He sprayed red paint first, close up so it went on in a big red blob. With the other can he used a fanning motion leaving a black speckled effect. When he was through, we all agreed it was art, and Stark and I hurried to get our cameras to snap some pictures.

The spraypaint had a preserving effect on the pig's head duded up. It didn't change for months. The unpainted pig's head, however, proceeded through its decaying cycle.

Unable to withstand gravity much longer, it flattened out gradually and turned a charcoal color, like a cake that fell and burned in the oven. One day it showed up in the alley next to our building, somehow now *clear across the street*, maybe brought over by a wild dog who coughed it up. Naturally, after lying a week or two underfoot of cars and trucks, it got squashed into a lump, flattened by a hundred tires riding over it, almost a new layer to the street like an asphalt patch filling a pot hole.

Finally, after six months or more, all that remained was a black circle staining the concrete sort of like an oil spot. But Stark and I knew that it was not an oil spot but a pig's head gone to its final resting place in the Sangamon ecosystem, remembered only by Stark and me.

The spraypainted pig's head withstood the rain, wind, and heat, and, being pickled, the microorganisms trying to chew their way out. It nonetheless disappeared one day, though; we still don't know to where.

Our theory about the pigs' heads' origins revolved around their being a joke, maybe put into some meatpacker's black metal lunch bucket. We also guessed that maybe a bum pulled them out of a dumpster behind one of the packinghouses, but he dumped them again, perhaps having second thoughts about pig's head soup for supper.

Regarding the disappearance of the spraypainted pig's head, a thought I had is that the Streets and Sanitation people came by and picked it up on one of their rare visits around the neighborhood.

"It could've been Animal Control, too," Stark said. "My uncle who works for Trees went out with them once. They collect abandoned rabid dogs and dead pigeons and shit."

I agreed that this was a good possibility, as good as any of the others. What I thought was the most likely was that the lone remaining pig's head got put back into another unlucky guy's lunch box—a better joke when they're spraypainted even than when they're fresh.

# 12 Geography of the Mind

I was aware of the word "Sangamon" long before I moved onto Sangamon Street. For instance, I heard the word from a friend of mine from high school days, whose sister attended Sangamon State University, located in Springfield, Illinois. As a long-time resident of Illinois, I was cognizant of the state's geography and therefore knew the name of the county that contains the state capitol: Sangamon. Finally, I learned in grade school that the rails which Lincoln split with his axe were used to build flat boats that floated up and down the river flowing through Springfield, the Sangamon.

While living on Sangamon Street I became interested in this unusual word, one it seemed I had heard all my life, so I sought out books that might tell me what the word meant. From a book describing the early history of Sangamon county, *Sugar Creek: Life on the Illinois Prairie*, by John Mack Farragher, I discovered that "Sangamon" was, as I suspected, an Indian word. Within the pages of *Sugar Creek* Farragher provides the etymology of "Sangamon":

> The word—which Americans first pronounced San-gamma, then Sangamo, and finally Sangamon—probably derived from the Algonquin *saginawa*, or "river's mouth," and was a cognate of other Algonquin river names like "Saginaw" and "Sagatuck."

Farragher continues by saying that certain white settlers who ended up in Sangamon country took liberties with this word's official definition out of an eagerness to convince prospective settlers (and probably themselves, too) of the beauty of the land and the quality of life there. One such settler, John Reynolds, wrote that "in the Pottawatomie language, Sangamon means 'the country where there is plenty to eat.' According to our parlance, it would be termed the land of milk and honey."

I repeated this definition to Stark one day, and he laughed his scoffing, one-snort, nobody-tells-me-anything laugh. He said, "That's not right. It should mean 'Land of truck fumes and pigs' heads.'"

Indeed, there does seem to be some differences of opinion as to what the word means. I talked to another person about it, somebody who actually lived on Sangamon the street, and therefore somebody who should know.

I had seen fairly often one certain bum roaming the neighborhood. He was Mexican-looking, had stringy black hair, and always wore the same set of clothes no matter if it were winter or summer: a brown and tan plaid felt shirt with too-short sleeves, and a pair of dingy blue jeans which hiked up his legs too far. One summer day, as I sat sunning myself in my chair out on the sidewalk in front of our building, he staggered by and showed an interest in the six-pack of Strohs beer that sat beside me. I decided to give him a beer, and maybe try to strike up a conversation. It turns out his name was José, or at least that's what his fellow bums called him on account of his Mexican looks. I found out, however, that in reality he was an Indian, and his full name was Joe Listening Rabbit. He said he lived at what was known around the neighborhood as the "Indian Docks," a bunch of abandoned docks located near the intersection of Kinzie and Milwaukee, where those of Native American descent made camp. I asked Joe if he knew what "Sangamon" meant.

He told me that the place first named Sangamon was the spot

in a cornfield above which floodwaters from the river would not rise during the spring.

Then he added that the word also could mean "to miss by a little." While out hunting, he explained, Indian men would not always bag every animal they set out to kill. Sometimes one of these hunters would spot a buck in a clearing in the woods, sneak up behind it, take careful aim with his bow and arrow, shoot, then watch the arrow miss and stick in the ground behind the deer which would dart away. Fellow braves could see that their companion followed all the traditionally taught methods for hunting deer and could recognize the bad break he got, for it happened to them from time to time as well. "Sangamon," one of them would say to the unlucky hunter, soothing words meaning "you missed the buck only by a little."

I thanked him for his taking time to talk with me, I gave him another beer, I wished him good luck, and I watched him stagger up to the corner, then turn west down Fulton Street, no doubt to shop around in the dumpsters outside the packing houses.

While living on Sangamon Street, I began to understand the full import of this word, and could see how language updates itself, changing to meet new conditions. We never hunted, of course, but we did miss things only by a little. Just as you would get to the top of the stairs and onto the L platform, you'd watch as the doors shut and the train pulled away. Or, walking to the bus, you'd watch from a quarter block away as your bus streaked past the bus stop. Or, when you were late for work and every second counted, you would enter the lobby of the skyscraper where you work and watch the elevator take off without you. All we could say when such things happened was "Sangamon."

After meeting a real-live Indian, I started to fancy myself as a frontiersman, which when you think about it, was absurd, because Sangamon didn't even approach my idea of unspoiled wilderness—you know, meadows, timberland, mountain ranges, water systems and clean skies. Instead, you could say that Sangamon was *oversettled*, like numerous patches of land throughout the world, where the population had exhausted the soil and extracted all the useful minerals, then moved on to continue the process someplace else. Still, I intuitively felt like some kind of pioneer; this feeling was reinforced one day when Stark informed me that the newspaper ad which originally lured him to Sangamon advertised the place as "perfect for urban pioneers." More than anything, the investigations into frontier life I soon conducted were designed to justify my rather vain belief that I was a singular individual living in a very special place.

I focused especially on Frederick Jackson Turner's celebrated essay, "The Frontier in American History," which I pulled up on microfilm at the Chicago Public Library. In that essay appear these lines:

> American social development has been continually beginning over again on the frontier. This perennial rebirth, this fluidity of American life, this expansion westward with its new opportunities, its continuous touch with the simplicity of primitive society, furnish the forces dominating American character.

Turner claims that the advancing frontier was the single most important aspect of American history and, as such, should provide the historian with fertile ground for interpreting the American past. Unfortunately, as Turner admits, only historians were left with any fertile ground to work with; the rest of us who were born after the closing of the frontier are stuck renting our homes and working for somebody else's benefit.

I can't resent this fate of mine too much, however, because I have the good sense to realize that you take potluck regarding when you arrive in the world. If there truly is a god, I can imagine him (or her) blindfolded, reaching into a fishbowl full of lottery numbers, pulling out a capsule, opening it, and announcing that all souls stamped with the number 1961 or 1776 or 1492, whichever is drawn, hereby are drafted to take their places in the world, and should report to the nearest birthing station. I guess I should be grateful to live in America during the twentieth century, when I compare my fate to that of luckless bastards like the cave people, medieval serfs, coastal Africans circa 1660, or Native Americans, who, in the closing of the frontier, had their homes stolen away. Nevertheless, I felt gypped; as an American, I had inherited this desire to conquer frontiers, but, with the frontier closed since 1890, I asked myself *what was left*?

Outer space was one possibility. But space travel in the 1980s was only for a select few—scientifically trained air force and army officers in tip-top physical shape—and not for lazy, dope-smoking assholes like me with degrees in the humanities.

Studying Turner, the acknowledged frontier expert, I happened on the answer to my question when I read the census bureau's definition of "frontier": "the margin of that settlement which has a density of two or more to the square mile." I thought about my situation left of the Loop: Stark and I were the only two inhabitants within a radius of four blocks or more. Given this definition, our neighborhood was indeed a type of frontier.

I compare Stark to that other first settler to Sangamon country, Robert Pulliam, a bona fide frontiersman about whom I learned when I read Farragher's book *Sugar Creek*. In 1817 Pulliam made the trek from the American Bottom region of southern Illinois, an area which stretched along the east bank of the Mississippi River, to what is now Sangamon County. Pulliam, who originally hailed from Kentucky, made his living by squatting on various parcels of land in Kentucky and southern Illinois. He arrived in Sangamon country with a small herd of cattle and pigs, which grazed on the tough, but life-sustaining prairie grass, and he tapped maple trees for sap. During his stay, he built a log house in the Indian style, where he cooked down the sap into syrup. He periodically returned to American Bottom to sell his fattened stock and his syrup, but, although the owner of a log house, he died without ever owning any land in Sangamon County.

Later, paying tribute to Pulliam for his groundbreaking efforts, the leading citizens of Sangamon County, who formed an Old Settlers' Society in 1849, dubbed him "the pioneer of Sangamon County." I imagine this caused certain people to choke on these words, because Pulliam sounds like a ne'er-do-well; according to Farragher, Pulliam, who, it should be noted, had a peg leg, liked "wrestling, animal baiting, and horse racing," and he had a reputation as a "pretty considerable" drinker and gambler. However, peg leg and all, the Old Settlers Society had to admire how Pulliam, the oldest settler of all, braved the wilds of Sangamon country, making a life for himself on his terms alone.

Like Robert Pulliam, Stark wanted to make a fresh start in life. At his previous address, in the Uptown neighborhood of Chicago, he bought a bunch of lead-lined room dividers and attempted to build a soundproof enclosure within his apartment, so he could practice his drums without disturbing his neighbors. Unfortunately, the neighbors still complained about the noise, causing him to pull up stakes and move to a place where nobody would close him in, where he could make as much noise as he damned well wanted to. He chose the West Loop. As with the early careers of nearly every pioneer before him, Stark had failed, but he wasn't defeated; he simply moved onward to better himself. Earlier pioneers, like Pulliam, moved to find better land and improve their economic situations; Stark moved in order to improve his musical skill.

Now, in the nineteenth century, the census only counted *settled* people on the frontier, and not the Indians who very definitely lived there, but who oftentimes lived nomadic lifestyles. People very much like the Indians, street people who wandered the streets and alleys, thriving off the land surrounding our loft, neighborhood natives if you will, preceded Stark and me, the first two *settlers* in Outer Bohemia. Like the Kickapoo Indians of Sangamon County, who, says Farragher, had a highly developed culture, "gathering, hunting, and fishing in seasonal cycles," but who looked to the settlers as savages, so too did the street people on Sangamon have a culture of their own, although to us their lives looked nasty and mean-spirited. They fished in dumpsters for every scrap of food they could lay their hands on, they hunted in alleys and along curbs for aluminum cans, and they gathered on street corners in bottle gangs, where two or more individuals would pitch in some change, buy some wine, and share the bottle.

With visions of frontier life floating around in my head, I used to look out the windows and behold the geography left of the Loop, this place of burned-out buildings, vacant lots choked with weeds, garbage piles, abandoned train tracks, and bombed-out cars. Looking across the street at the windows of Zimmerman Brush Company, sometimes for hours at a time, long enough once to see a glass pane spontaneously fall out of its frame and shatter on the street, I'd pine away thinking about the lucky devils who built the first foundations on Sangamon Street, back when there was grass, when the air was free of truck fumes, when somebody could sit outside in a chair, on a porch for real, not on the damned sidewalk, hemmed in by telephone poles and parked cars butting up against each other like multicolored billy goats. In short, I yearned to see what Sangamon Street looked like before there was such a thing as Skid Row.

Miraculously, I received such a glimpse. One day, while visiting the Chicago Historical Society, I ran across a 4-foot by 8-foot map in a gilt frame entitled "Chicago, 1857." The map was genuine; on the bottom border an inscription by the mapmaker showed the date as 1857. Interestingly, the map was not the conventional two-dimensional, airborne-shot type of map, but rather a three-dimensional map drawn and lithoed in perspective. Being over a century old, yellowing had diminished the blues of Lake Michigan and the Chicago river, the greens of the parks and yards, the ochres of the streets and railroad rights of way, and the reds and grays of houses and public buildings.

A broad lap of blue, the lake, washed across the bottom, with a few juts of flesh-colored land here and there where lighthouses stood. A few boats dotted the lake, wood-looking things that reminded me of giant barrels floating on their sides, but most boats and ships, rigging all atangle, crowded the focal point of the map: the confluence of the various branches of the Chicago River. At the time the riverfront must have been like the Dan Ryan Expressway of today.

Like today, gigantic structures crowded the shore, except in 1857 storehouses and cylindrical grain elevators loomed over the water, instead of the present-day skyscrapers. Train tracks were everywhere, looping around the buildings, then cutting south down the lakeshore. Enclosed between the lake and the north and south branches of the river were clusters of commercial buildings; each street amongst these buildings was labeled and called pretty much what it's called today. The county courthouse at Randolph and La Salle was especially prominent, its clock scowling in every direction the official Chicago time.

Jumping across the river, about halfway up the map by now, my eyes zeroed in on a couple of blocks between Clinton Street and "Halstead Street." This I realized was the Haymarket, a street wider than any other on the map, and wide still today, but different then, for a big meeting hall with a bell tower was planted in the middle of it. The map's legend identified this building as "Wal Market Hall."

Three blocks west of Halsted Street, or about three-quarters of the way up the map, I saw, sure enough, Sangamon Street. Counting with my finger two blocks north, above and to the right of the Haymarket, I found the very block where we used to live. All that stood on the block way back when were a large, two-story farmhouse-looking structure and a few small outbuildings.

They definitely had it better in 1857: instead of cavernous warehouses, a bunch of farmhouses were scattered along Sangamon Street, each with practically a whole block of grass and gardens to itself. Across the street from our block, where the brush factory was located, there was, judging from stacks of wood planks randomly dropped on the block, a lumber company. What especially struck me about the area then was the extraordinary number of trees lining the gravel streets, trees long cut down, probably sawed into beams to fill the city's need for more and more homes, then burned up during the Chicago Fire.

Just six blocks west of Sangamon, almost to the very top of the map, the city ended at Ada Street. The streets going west simply faded into the vanishing point in the middle of a thick forest on the horizon, like the streets in small towns where I've lived end at a creek or a cornfield. Beyond that: blue sky and clouds.

Thanks to the Fire, which burned up all evidence of land ownership recorded in Chicago before 1871, I will never know who the occupants of 210 North Sangamon were in 1857. The only information I could find concerning the hazy origins of Sangamon was that the lands bordered by Kinzie, Halsted, Ann and Madison Streets were deeded to a man named Philo Carpenter on August 18, 1836. What Carpenter actually did with his property must forever remain a mystery. I can only guess that the lands surrounding Sangamon underwent a process something like the following:

One hundred sixty-five years ago, ambitious men eyed the wooded area now called Sangamon Street, and gradually they built homes and factories, according to the developers' respective notions of improvement. What a hundred years of industrialization and then de-industrialization accomplished was to create what I called the "Post-Industrial Urban Apocalypse."

But, as with any apocalypse in either the eastern religions, where practitioners have the foresight to see an apocalypse as a recurring thing, or in Christianity, which sees only one at the end of history, there is the element purification, of erasing the land and then writing history all over again. Put another way, like some of those locations in the Middle East in which new civilizations built on top of the old, Stark and I were sifting through the rubble of our neighborhood and, with a little mumbo jumbo, transforming its geography in the mind's eye. Carl Sandburg must have been thinking the same thing when he wrote the lines stenciled on the wall above the map that I saw at the Historical Society:

> Put the city up; tear the city down; put it up again; let us find a city.

True, there will never again be pin oaks, jackpines, maples, walnuts, prairie grass or wild flowers thriving left of the Loop. But I could look out the loft's windows and see telephone poles and light poles instead of trees. I could look at the vacant lot across the street, which we called the Sangamon Prairie, and see cardboard boxes roll by like tumbleweeds. And although we didn't have pheasants, elk or bear, we did have wildlife of sorts: squirrels, pigeons, rats and wild dogs.

Once, though I'm not sure if this truly happened, or if I dreamt it in my sleep and remembered it as really happening, I heard a distant honking which caused me to look up at the sky. Overhead I saw the "V" shape of Canadian geese flying south. I realized that up in those timeless regions where geese and imagination fly the lay of the land looked the same.

# 13 | Bank Business

Late one night after work, when I walked through the big steel sliding door into our loft, a big red dog racing out of the loft about bowled me over. "Grab him!" Stark yelled. This I did, cuffing him by the collar, expecting the dog to rear up any second and bite off my tits. Instead, the dog sat down politely, and with me still grasping his collar, he relaxed, panting and staring through the doorway at the landing's far wall.

My first inclinations were that the dog there on Sangamon was cool; still, I wanted some explanation regarding his moving in. "Do you know this dog?" I asked Stark, knowing full well he must, because he still was awake way past his 9:30 bedtime, and he had this shrugging "I got talked into it" air about him suggesting that he waited up to explain something to me. This something, of course, was the dog.

"That's Lord Cornwallis," said Stark. "He's my mom's dog. We have to watch him while she's in San Francisco for a week at a dog show."

"If she's at a dog show, then why is he here?"

"He's only ten-months old. He's still a puppy."

"He looks pretty full-grown to me."

"Sure, he's full grown, but she says he still has 'a puppy's constitution.' She took four dogs as it was, and she didn't want to take him, too. Said 'he's like an extra suitcase with legs on a trip' because he's too young yet to compete."

I twirled the dog around by the collar and released him back into the loft. He ran to a spot beside the folding chair in which Stark was seated, directly facing our groty old gas heater, and carefully sat himself. Once set, his ears, which in his previous excitement pricked up like switchblades, lay down. Since there was still a spring chill in the air, I grabbed the other of our two folding chairs and sat before the heater alongside Stark and the dog.

Stark filled me on the story: Stark's mother had to make this dog show trip, but the dog sitter she planned on, a neighbor woman who had cared for the dogs before in her absence, was walking in her yard the previous week and stepped on a nail that punctured her foot clean through. Stark was the only other person available whom his mother trusted to dog sit. Problem was, she wanted him to stay at her house, way out in the western suburbs of Chicago, for six days. "There's no way. It'd take an hour and a half each way to work," he explained. "So I talked her into letting him stay with me. She was a little bit leery at first, but she gave in, so the dog's here and thankfully I'm not there."

"What did you say his name was?"

"Lord Cornwallis."

"You mean like the British general who lost the Battle of Yorktown?"

"I guess. My mom's into those Anglo-sounding names."

"That's what she actually calls him, 'Lord Cornwallis?'"

As if to prove a point, when I said the dog's name, his ears perked up again, but his eyes remained fixed on a spot on the opposite wall.

"I don't know if I can call him that. That's not a dog's name, you know, like Fido or Buster or Rug."

"Rug?" Stark asked.

"Yeah, my old dog Rug. Rest his soul."

"I don't think Rug sounds any more like a dog's name than Lord Cornwallis, but I don't know. I guess other people besides breeders like my mom name their dogs some corny things."

"That's it. We can call him Corny. Hey Corny!" I shouted at the dog.

The dog sat there and tilted his head up slightly and barked not-very-threateningly at the wall. Still sitting, he continued to stare at the object of his bark, either something real that he saw there in the bricks or, more likely, some imagined dog thing. I'm sure he fully knew I was addressing him, but he was ignoring me all the same.

"He doesn't answer to that," Stark observed. "Watch this. Yo! Wally!"

The dog stood up and turned around to acknowledge his caller; then he sat down again and stared up at Stark for a while rather than at the wall.

"Wally it is," I said.

"Check this out—I tried it out on him earlier. Wally! lie down!" The dog sank down on all fours, rested his chin on the rug, and closed his eyes. After awhile the conversation tapered off and died as the three of us sat by the groty old gas heater. Fried from long days, Stark and I stared at the relaxing blue and orange jets, watching them flicker and dance, almost like we had a fireplace and owned a dog we could sit with and enjoy our peace.

****

The next day I rose about noon. Wally was lying on the rug in front of the gas heater. Seeing me emerge from my room, he sat up and watched me expectantly, but I didn't pay him much attention beyond saying, "Morning, Wally," and checking to make sure he had enough water in the dog dish Stark's mother sent with him. I really couldn't spend time with him, because I had important business to get underway that day; we received our paychecks the night before, and I had to visit the Skid Row Bank in order to cash it. I figured I could hang out with Wally when I returned, and maybe even take him out for a walk around the neighborhood, which, with all the meatpacking businesses, surely must have been dog heaven. Already dressed and planning to skip breakfast, I left the loft saying, "So long, Wally."

Our bank was located at the cross roads of Skid Row, Halsted and Madison. Like fortresses of old, where kings hoarded their gold, it was surrounded by attendant ramshackle structures: flea bag hotels, liquor stores, greasy spoons, pawn shops, a mission, and other assorted store fronts long since boarded up. A steady stream of derelict-looking types, none of whom ever seemed to walk into the bank, let alone in a straight line, doddered by its doors or waited beneath its Romanesque facade for the bus. On a couple of occasions, I'd seen people reclining out front on the sidewalk, sleeping off their drunkenness. From all outward indicators in the surrounding neighborhood, I gathered that the bank's depositors must have been of an ancient class: absentee lords of a land where the landowners taxed their tenants into penurious dissipation.

Cutting through a vacant lot in my approach to the bank, I suddenly found myself in its shadow and paused to look up at the six-story-tall edifice, the most impressively ornate in the neighborhood. Before walking through the polished brass revolving door, I observed a guard swaggering along the bank's front window; without even breaking his stride, he kicked the shoes of a guy sitting on the sidewalk against the bank's granite wall and told him to get up and move along.

Once inside, I got into line. One of the Men With Important Titles, or "M-WITs" as Stark called them, must have experienced a bank line brainstorm, for I discovered the bank recently had installed a new system. Rather than getting into one of the many lines forming before two walls of windows, you walked to the end of one line that zigzagged between velvet ropes strung between brass posts. In addition to resenting the arrogance of the bank guard and his dealings with the guy outside, I suddenly resented the arrogance of corralling me with these ropes. I went "MOO!" through my hands, a gesture that cracked up the guy in front of me, but which drew glares from several tellers peering out from behind the iron bars blocking their windows.

Since it was a Friday, the universal payday, there were about twenty people in line ahead of me and a rapidly increasing number stepping up behind. I counted eleven windows making transactions and the usual five or six more which were closed. To my surprise, the line moved along pretty briskly; to the credit of the M-WIT who thought it up, the new system appeared faster than the old. But when I became about number twelve in line, six of the eleven tellers put up "Next window please" signs, leaving, I presumed, for lunch. "MAN!" I shouted a moment later, because the line already had begun to drag. This expression of disgust registered with the remaining tellers; several glared at me once again.

"Next," a teller announced after about twenty-five or thirty minutes. I walked up to the window, endorsed my check, and handed it and my savings account passbook to the teller.

All I had was a savings account. With its simple addition and subtraction, all calculated by computers at the bank, a savings account was much easier to keep track of my money than a checking account, which, when all the figuring and ciphering was left in my hands, inevitably led to overdrafts.

After looking at me distastefully, the teller, who was named Hector Gonzalez, according to his nameplate, turned his back to me and spent an extra-long time verifying my signature in the card file on the counter behind him. Upon turning again to face me, he punched the keys to his computer super-fast, then glanced to see what effect this impressive sleight-of-hand display had on me. He stared down at the computer screen another half-minute or so. Finally, he delivered his verdict.

"I'm sorry, but I can't cash this check. You don't have any money in the account to cover it," he said.

"Yeah I know. It's payday. What can I say? I live hand to mouth like everybody else around here."

"It should take about five days to clear. If you want to come back then . . ."

"Look, Hector, the check's written on the biggest bank in Chicago. It's a good check."

"I'll get the head teller. He has to approve it."

"You do that." Through the iron bars I watched Hector walk behind the row of tellers and through a door.

Standing there, waiting for Hector to bring back his M-WIT, I seethed at the audacity of some bank questioning my integrity.

Hector came back through the door with the Head Teller, who I felt sure would turn out to be a real trout brain, just like every other M-WIT.

"May I help you?" Trout Brain asked.

"He tells me you can't cash this check. That's not acceptable. I mean, I have to eat, you know?"

"Our policy is to wait for the check to clear, but I'll go ahead and authorize giving you fifty dollars."

"That's so big of you." He initialed the check, and Hector handed me two twenties and a ten.

"Come back in five days," Trout Brain said. "The full amount should be available by then. Thanks for your cooperation," he said, too cheerfully.

****

My anger at the bank subsided when Wally greeted me at the door upon my return home. He ran right up to me, panting, his tongue reminding me of a hand and wrist extending to shake hands. The night before Stark had said that he would feed and walk the dog in the morning, and I should take him out once before I left for work in the afternoon. In the combative state I was in after my trip to the bank, I figured that walking Wally would be just the therapy I needed. After snapping the leash Stark's mother left onto his collar, we charged out the door.

The weeds growing up through the cracks along our curb were an immediate hit with Wally. He sniffed through the weeds, probably picking up the scent of old Burger King and Kentucky Fried Chicken bags Stark and I had dumped when getting out of friends' cars after trips to fast food drive-up windows. Being spring, our trash was submerged in weeds, but during the barren winter previous, Stark and I noticed that such refuse clogged our gutter the entire width of our building. I objected at first when Stark dropped his bags full of burger wrappers; eventually, however, I gave in to Stark's justification—"When on Sangamon, do as the Sangamonians do"—and I commenced adding to the gutter garbage by throwing my trash there, too.

Finished with our gutter, Wally towed me across the street to check out the Sangamon Prairie, the name Stark and I gave to a vacant lot across the street. The Sangamon Prairie was overgrown with weeds, like all the vacant lots left of the Loop except for the ones heaping with trash piles or dirt mounds. Watching his furious sniffing amongst the sparse weeds, it dawned on me that Wally was in the mood for nature, with a capital "N", surroundings he was accustomed to out in the suburbs, with their parks, trails and forest preserves. I unclipped his leash and let him run free for a while.

After ten minutes or so, I called out to Wally, and he dutifully trotted back. I put on his leash and knelt beside him in order to pet him. Only I didn't really know where to start. Stark informed me the night before that Wally was a Rhodesian ridgeback, a breed I wasn't familiar with; however, in daylight it was plain why his ancestors got that name, for he had a ridge running from the nape of his neck to the beginning of his stringy tail. The way the fur reversed direction from the rest of his back, it looked like somebody squeezed a tube of mousse down his spine and teased the fur up with a brush. Not certain which way was the right way, and not wanting to pet a dog the wrong way, I settled on petting only his head and chest.

When we returned to the loft, I was concerned that Wally didn't do his business, didn't even lift his leg during our walk. I sensed he needed to relieve himself, because he paced around the loft like he was feeling a little edgy, instead of his normal behavior, which was to sit like a gentleman. But I figured it was his tough luck if he didn't go. "You had ample opportunity," I said to him, scoldingly; he responded with a sheepish look. After showering and packing my lunch, during which time I tossed Wally a couple of scraps of chipped beef from my sandwich, I gave him one final pat on the head and left for work.

****

"Wally shit on the floor," Stark said immediately upon realizing it was me on the phone. I had ducked out of the proofreading room at Sickly & Caustic and called him from a conference room, where there was more privacy.

"Sorry, but I took him out for a walk. We were out forty-five minutes, and he never went the whole time."

"He doesn't go on his own," Stark explained.

"What do you mean?"

The tone of Stark's voice was bordering on impatience. "You have to tell him to."

"Huh?"

"That's the way my mom trains all her dogs. It keeps them from taking a shit at an embarrassing moment like a dog show finale."

"I'm sorry, Stark, but I've never heard of any dog that waited for permission. I mean, what do you say to him?"

"'Go ahead.' That's what my mom used to say to her dogs when I was growing up. It worked this morning when I took him out."

"That's the damnedest thing I ever heard of. A dog that's so well trained he goes on command. Wild!"

I proceeded to change the subject and described to Stark my miserable time at the bank earlier that day.

"Remember our bank when we were in college?" asked Stark, suddenly lighting up at the prospect of bad-mouthing banks.

"Remember one time when we tried their drive-in branch? And they wouldn't let you withdraw from your account in the drive-through, because you had to go inside for that? And we didn't want to, so we went ahead to the grocery store, but we were so broke all we bought was chili? And we drove back to the bank? And I opened up a can of chili with my pocketknife and dumped it into their damn pneumatic tube? And then you shot it back and we sped off? Remember that?"

"That was cool. Actually, did I ever tell you the coolest thing I ever saw happen in a bank? It was when I was a kid. I went with my dad on a Saturday morning because they had Saturday hours. In their drive-through they used to give the kids candy, and if you brought your dog, they'd give it a dog treat. So I'd get a sucker, and Rug got a dog biscuit. Well, for some reason, my dad had to go inside and talk to somebody, so he took the dog and me with him. He did things like that. I remember a couple of times we went inside K-Mart with the dog.

"Anyway, Rug was kind of skittish around little kids, and there was this little girl with her mother behind us in line. She reached down to pet him, and he must've freaked because he took a shit right there on the floor of the bank. I still remember the little girl saying, 'Look, Mama! The dog just did number two.'"

Stark and I let out huge guffaws at the punch line of my story, one I'm certain I'd told ten times before. Then, as if the nerve endings of our brains were spliced together via the phone wires, we simultaneously asked each other the very same question: "You know what we ought to do . . . ?"

****

The following Friday around noon, Stark, Wally and I found ourselves walking south on Halsted Street. Stark met Wally and me on his lunch hour so that all three of us could pay a visit to the Skid Row Bank. As we walked, we hatched our plan.

"So you're sure he hasn't gone yet?"

"Positive."

"Think they'll let him inside the bank?"

"If I'm alone I can talk them into it. But if we're seen together, they'll make one of us stay outside with the dog."

"Then I better hang out here a couple of minutes." He sat down on an empty, upside-down cardboard box somebody had left behind on the sidewalk. "I'll see you in a few."

As I walked the remaining couple of blocks to the bank, Wally kept pausing and looking around at me, almost pleading with me to let him stop and do his business. "Don't worry, Wally," I assured him. "You'll get your chance real soon." I hoped I wasn't treating Wally too cruelly, because I knew what it was like when I had to hold it in. But I also knew that Stark's mother surely would have put Wally through the paces at a dog show; I excused myself by believing that Stark and I were giving Wally his first test as a public performer.

After taking a deep breath, I said, "Ready, Wally," and we two entered the bank through the revolving door. Just like I expected, a security guard pounced on us. "There aren't any dogs allowed in here," he said. "You're going to have to tie him up outside."

"I'm sorry, but I can't do that. He's a purebred Rhodesian ridgeback. You ever hear of them?"

"No . . ."

"They're real valuable. If I left him outside, somebody would steal him. They could get a couple hundred bucks from the right person."

The guard frowned at the dog and me, but in that frown I detected compassion for dogs sneaking through, a feeling which betrayed his tool-of-the-capitalist-class sensibilities. Nonetheless, he appeared to stand firm. "I'm sorry, but I just can't let you in the bank with a dog."

"C'mon!" I begged. "I absolutely have to take care of some business today. He's trained real well by a professional breeder. He won't bite anybody."

"Can't you lock him in your car?"

"I'm on foot. Look, there's nothing else I can do with him. Try and pet him. He's a real friendly dog."

The guard reached down and cautiously patted Wally on the head. Then, probably intimidated by the ridge on his back, he patted Wally's sides, saying, "There's a good dog. Good dog."

Finally, the guard relented. "I guess he won't hurt nobody. Go on along. But if anybody hassles you, you tell 'em that Jim the guard says it's okay by him."

"Thanks, Jim." Wally and I left Jim the guard and took our places in line. Surprisingly, we ended up fourth, even though it was Friday at lunchtime. Waiting there I began to feel anxious about my upcoming stunt. To dispel my anxieties, I focused my attention on the Corinthian columns, examining the gold-layered acanthus leaves at their tops. In typically arrogant fashion, the builders of the Skid Row Bank plagiarized the Roman style, which the Romans in turn appropriated at spear point from the Greeks. This reminded me of the outrageous tribute the bank exacted from me: two dollars per transaction when I withdrew money from my savings account, which they turned around and paid out as interest to some big depositor's account. With the help of my faithful comrade Wally, I would pay them back for all the suspicious eyeballings I received over the years, and was receiving even then from bank tellers who disapproved of me and my dog.

Seeing Stark out of the corner of my eye snapped me out of my reverie. When Wally spotted him, he began to wag his tail, but nobody but me seemed to notice. All of a sudden it was my turn to approach the next available window.

"That's a funny-looking dog," the teller said, a young woman whose cheeks were swollen on account of a severe acne problem.

"He's a Rhodesian ridgeback. They use them to hunt lions."

"I hope you're not going to use him to help you rob this bank!" she said, then laughed.

"Actually, he's here to help me close my account," I said, handing her my passbook.

The teller, who didn't have a plaque displaying her name, only an empty sign holder, went about her job. Thankfully, my check from the previous week had cleared, but she still had to have Trout Brain approve the transaction. While she was away from the window, I decided that she was okay as bank employees go; her laugh and her genuine disappointment upon hearing I was closing my account amounted to a refreshing dose of humanity and trust in a hard-hearted, paranoid bank environment. I just couldn't bring myself to have Wally do his thing in front of her window. When the teller returned she stamped my passbook "account closed," and she counted out four hundred or so dollars. I thanked her and proceeded to scope out an M-WIT to terrorize with Wally.

I walked directly to a man who sat behind a gigantic, green marble desk. His nameplate read "Mr. Craig Sokup, Assistant Vice President"; I figured he possessed an important enough title.

"Yes?" he asked, looking up. His glasses were covered with dandruff, like somebody sprinkled salt from a shaker all over them.

"Yeah. I wanted to tell you that I just closed my account because you have a bunch of goddamn, dumb ass rules here. I'd rather stash my money in a goddamn underwear drawer."

"There's no cause to use that kind of language here."

"I'll use any kind of language I want. You want to hear me say 'fuck'? Okay, here goes. FUCK."

"If you can't conduct yourself properly, then I'll have to call a guard and have him escort you out of the bank."

"Go ahead," I said. Wally's ears perked up when he heard these magical words. He looked up at me with a curious expression; if he could have talked, he would have said, "In here? Are you sure?"

Sokup, as well, looked blankly at me, as if to say, "Come again?" No doubt he ruled the roost and was not accustomed to somebody squawking back. "I'll just do that," he finally declared, his attention once again focused on me.

"Go ahead," I said again, this time more to Wally than to Sokup. Told twice, Wally could make no mistake about the irregular circumstances—he hunched down, and, smack in the center of a two-foot square of marble tile, he shat.

"Ooops. It looks like my dog had some bank business of his own to take care of," I remarked. Stark, fifteen feet to my right, erupted into peals of laughter.

"You did that on purpose!" said Sokup. "I saw you. You said 'go ahead' to the dog. I could have you arrested for vandalism."

"It'd be hard to prove. I mean, whoever's heard of a dog that goes on cue?"

"You just clean it up and get the hell out of my bank," he said, pointing grandiloquently at the door.

"You heard the man." It was Jim the guard's voice. Looking closely at his face to determine how serious my trouble was, I saw his cheek and lip muscles wrestle. His cheeks, which fought hard to smile, appeared to gain the advantage over his lips, which fought equally hard to frown.

"Whatever you say, Jim," I said, slipping my passbook out of its plastic sleeve. Then I stooped over and scooped up Wally's mess between the fake leather covers.

"Now you take that and get out," Sokup said. But it was too late—I already had leaned over his desk and deposited the fouled passbook into a tall steel wastebasket beside his chair. I headed for the door. In my wake I heard Sokup asking Jim why he had allowed Wally to enter the bank in the first place.

"He seemed like a friendly enough dog. Sometimes they get antsy and can't help themselves," Jim explained.

Stark met Wally and me in the vacant lot across the street from the bank. "Grace under pressure," he said, describing how our team, the West Loop Ridgebacks, was victorious over their team, the Bank Buffoons.

"On the way home I'm going to stop at a butcher shop on Randolph Street and treat Wally to a pound of raw hamburger," I announced. Before that time, however, and before Stark returned to work, we got down on hands and knees in order to congratulate Wally by petting him, hugging him, kissing him, and rubbing his belly and chest for close to half an hour.

# 14 Left of the Loop: The Poem

When I first went to live with Stark left of the Loop, I called myself a poet, although only nervously because I had never published a book nor made any money from writing. True, I had published in a couple of little magazines, but when people asked what I did, I told them I proofread at the law firm of Sickly & Caustic, keeping my artistic ambitions to myself. Since I worked at night, I spent my days shut inside the loft trying to write a poem about the material I had at hand. After awhile my poem went like this:

***Left of the Loop***

My roommate and I
take it for granted,
living where we do,
that we can revel
in our madness, untouched.
It scares away guests . . .

The walls are brick
and painted peeling blue.
Ghosts seemingly
drift in and out
as if into clouds.

The L shoots us home.
It hurtles and tilts,
bumps us off of people
we plot against all day
from street level up
to the ninety-ninth floor.

It creeps, it slithers in
and rises up so much
it caves our stomachs in:
Truck Pollution.
They park late at night—
big diesels, panel trucks—
all stuffed with meat
that feeds a million mouths;
and all huff and puff
and blow us out of bed.

Wild dogs (one limps) rampage
after scraps the bums have left.
Wandering forever,
they bark and chew their growls,
snap at each other's heels.
We call the pound before they bite.

The picture is snowy
outside those windows—
it dusts in every crack,
every crevice of this place,
this body.

The pigs' heads someone dumped
on the sidewalk as a joke
will probably haunt us
for the rest of our days.

Our view is of a chute
that spits out bones,
ribs, skulls and innards
of countless cows.
It scares away guests . . .

So late at night, alone,
my roommate and I play ball,
tossing it, whipping it,
bouncing it off of walls,
catching it while tripping
over where the floor

wrenches up, and if
a window breaks or a lamp
is punched around a bit,
we laugh. We laugh hard.
We cry we laugh so hard.
We laugh. Hard.

This was an effort, I now realize, which goes far to explain the fistful of rejection slips I kept receiving in the mail from poetry magazines.

However, through a classic example of knowing the right people, the poem was published after all, the only piece of writing I published while living left of the Loop. One Sunday afternoon I showed my poem to a couple of band hangers-on who claimed to publish a rude, anarchist zine. They were peace-promoting skinhead types who showed up to band practice with Wanda; in addition to producing their zine they played in a hardcore punk band called Commercial Fodder.

At any rate, "Left of the Loop" appeared in a magazine titled, aptly enough, *Commercial Fodder*. The magazine itself sported a hand-made look—the text was typewritten, not typeset; the pages were photocopied, some quite crookedly; the cover, including lettering, was hand-drawn; and the volume was bound with black electrical tape and staples. The issue actually sold, on consignment, in about a dozen bookstores and record stores around Chicago, although it was the only issue I ever saw, and probably just as well, because it was mostly filled with dadaist drivel. Still, I appreciated its publication, and I hereby make grateful acknowledgment to Oleo and Ken, wherever they may be.

# 15 The Big Steel Door: An Allegory

The big wide sliding steel door keeps out intruders. And, with no fire escape, would seal us in in case a fire broke out. It's six feet wide and six feet high, three inches thick, like armor plate. Like on a boxcar, you open it by throwing down a latch, slide the door to the right, cock your hip for momentum and then shove from the shoulder. A padlock, the kind they shoot bullets through on television to prove the lock will stay locked, seals the door shut tight. But even a door like this can be broken down with a battering ram, or walked through like a ghost, or its lock picked clean as teeth.

One night, when I was off gallivanting, Stark lay up in his sleeping loft, I imagine on his back, knees up and crossed. He was wearing headphones plugged into his Walkman. He listened to Phil Spector's Christmas Album, sealing himself in by that wall of sound.

After awhile his unit clicked off, but he was too dissipated to flip the tape and listen to the second side. He woke up after a period of nodding off, and then he climbed down the ladder in a too-long trek to eat a snack of grape jelly on saltine crackers. He especially liked a layer of butter to squeeze out from under the jelly when he chose this combination, because the butter soothed a throat scorched from years of swallowing truck fumes.

When he gave the kitchen bulb a slight twist, the light, spotlight-fashion, flashed onto a pile of half our things stacked up by the door which stood wide open. There was his tape recorder boom box, a guitar amp, a guitar, an upside-down footstool, a small portable TV, a frying pan, a tape measure, a small table lamp, his Swiss army knife, a shoe box full of pewter chess pieces, two cans of paint we used to paint out all the dumb sayings people came and wrote on the walls, a whole box of plastic garbage can liners bought the day before, and a box of acrylic paints together with the drawing pad Stark had left empty, because he was too dissipated the week he bought the painting stuff to sit down and paint. Topping off the pile there were six boxes of macaroni and cheese and an almost full plastic gallon jug of two percent milk that still was cold. It seems somebody came in to clean us out while Stark lay sleeping, and when he got up, the person or persons unknown must have split town. They piled everything by the door first, so then it would be easy to sneak the stuff right out the big wide sliding steel door.

Too bad all that energy the robber brought to bear on his snatching scheme was a big fat waste. No whiskey or wine as a payoff for working and making a little money in order to support the lifestyle lived by one of the neighborhood's outdoor inhabitants.

When I asked how somebody could have gotten through the big steel door to take out all that stuff, Stark remarked that not only was he too dissipated to flip the tape he was listening to, but he was too dissipated to thread the lock through the latch from the inside. "The door was way over there," he explained.

# 16 Ghost of the Guy Who Threw the Haymarket Bomb

One May night, back in the days before Stark bought his van, we were walking south on Halsted Street, on our way to Greektown where we planned to buy our dinner at Zorba's Restaurant. Stark said he was going to order a gyros plate; my lips smacked in anticipation of buying myself the perch fillet sandwich. At $1.75 it was the best deal, because instead of a McDonaldsesque square of ground-up fish, you got an actual fillet that extended beyond the ends of a hot dog bun. Stark carried along his boom box which blared out a demo tape that he and The Strangers had recently made.

"Hear how Rudy the Roach is dragging there?" he asked, not expecting an answer.

Suddenly, as we were about to cross Randolph Street, something like an oversized acetylene torch flame flared up across the intersection.

"What the hell is that?" Stark asked, startled by the column of blue flame.

"I don't know. Maybe a gas main burst," I said.

"Should we check it out?"

"I don't know," I said. "Sometimes it's best to leave stuff like that alone. You wouldn't want your face burned off, would you?"

But we walked across the street despite our doubts, drawn as we were to this weird, fiery plume.

"I've seen some strange shit around the neighborhood," Stark said, "but I never saw any shit like that." The light by then had coalesced into a very definite form that was floating about three feet off the ground.

"Stark, I think it's like a ghost," I said as the form came further into focus the closer to it we walked.

"What do we do?" Stark asked while reaching down to stop the tape.

"It can't be; there's no such thing," I said. And yet there we were—face to face with a ghost.

The ghost didn't seem directly to threaten us, so we stood there in front of it, agape, our senses nevertheless recording every particular. The overall form glowed and bobbed up and down. Its outlines were human, at least insofar as the head, neck and shoulders were human. Beneath its shoulders and arms, however, the form ended in a gooey curlicue. Off the tip of this curlicue flaming drips were dropping to the sidewalk, where they promptly burned out. The sizzling sound this made, and the four to five second intervals, reminded me of how grease from hamburgers cooked on a grill drips down into the coals. The smell enveloping the area where we stood definitely was not barbecue, though; rather, it was one I didn't recognize. The nearest approximation I could think of was burning hair.

Curly locks and muttonchops surrounded the ghost's face. He wore a white shirt with an open tabbed collar and a linen vest that hung off his shoulders, clothes I figured were from the nineteenth century. His trunk, clothes and all, melted into this flash-fried curlicue.

"Holy shit!" Stark whispered, as the eyes of the ghost, which previously were closed, opened. I suddenly had abdominal cramps, the pins and needles kind which normally precede diarrhea.

When he looked as though he was about to speak, I frantically waved at Stark to get him to surreptitiously tape record whatever was said. He slowly fingered down the side of his boom box to push in the play and record buttons, all the while never taking his eyes off the apparition. What follows is a transcription of Stark's recording; a paranormal psychologist at Northwestern University since has declared it to be the only authentic instance of a ghost talking on tape. He even wrote a journal article about it, which has brought Stark and me a small measure of notoriety, but no money yet—I can't be sure that there was any conspiracy, but I think the lack of offers from the mass media to cover our story is due to the unpopularity of certain political beliefs the ghost expresses.

GHOST. You are dressed in the manner of workingmen. In what trades do you work?

STARK. Ah, uh, I'm a computer operator.

GHOST. A computer? Is that a new type of machine?

STARK. It's, uh, like a typewriter.

GHOST. Ah, yes. And you?

SPUNGKDT. Umm, uh, I'm a proofreader.

GHOST. An honorable profession. Do you work in a printing house?

SPUNGKDT. Law firm.

GHOST. Bah! I've got nothing good to say concerning the law.

SPUNGKDT. Neither do I.

STARK. Y-you a ghost?

GHOST. Indeed I am. It truly is ironic that I, a man who spent his entire life scoffing at the supernatural, have ended up in death as a ghost.

SPUNGKDT. W-why are you here?

GHOST. I'm here, so far as I can glean, to atone for a grave misdeed. Ghosts bring to mind all manner of devils, gods and hobgoblins. But neither devil nor god has spoken to me. Rather,

I have some vague feeling intruding on my being which has alerted me to my present fate: that I'm damned to haunt and roam Haymarket Square.

STARK & SPUNGKDT. B-but w-what d-did y-you d-do?

GHOST. I am the villain that threw the bomb into the delegation of police at what came to be known as the "Haymarket Affair"—one hundred and two years ago tonight.

STARK. I wish I could line up all the cops who've hassled me and toss a bomb at their knees.

GHOST. By this statement, and yours a moment ago regarding the law, I believe we all three share a distaste for the local constabulary.

SPUNGKDT. Them, my boss, our landlady, the phone company, and especially snotty tellers at the bank.

STARK. They're all out to screw you.

GHOST. A conglomeration of the very men of whom you speak once caused my throat to swell in anger much as your throats are swelling now. I'm quite saddened to hear that such corrupt and evil men live in your day, one hundred years into the future.

STARK. They always have and always will.

GHOST. There is a tone of cynicism in your words.

STARK. The 1980s are cynical times. Look who's president.

GHOST. I see we haven't yet abolished that office. Pray, who is the president?

STARK. You don't know?

GHOST. History ended for me at my death, so I have no memory of time passing after that unfortunate event.

SPUNGKDT. I can't bring myself to say his name. He was a movie actor at one time. Can you believe that?

GHOST. I see. A handsome devil. A handsome devil named Harding was president when I died. He was a man, incidentally, who turned back the calendar to those rapacious days surrounding the Haymarket Affair. After the revolution in Russia, I thought workingmen everywhere would throw off their chains to assume their rightful places as rulers of their own lives. This hasn't been the case?

STARK. Not hardly. Say! Let's hear about you throwing that bomb.

SPUNGKDT. Yeah. And what's your name, anyway? They never found out who threw the bomb, right?

GHOST. With a mixture of pride and shame I present myself: my name is Jacob Kallman. Directly across this square, over on Des Plaines Street, was the location of my infamous deed. After that pirate Captain Bonfield had his men chase down on horseback and shoot those strikers at McCormick Reaper, some individuals from anarchist circles called a meeting to be held at the Haymarket. A mob of around one or two thousand, myself included, gathered to hear August Spies and Albert Parsons, two leaders of the anarchist movement, speak.

Around a quarter past ten the last speaker, a German named Fielden, hastily ended his talk when a great gust of wind and rain blew up. As he descended from the speakers' wagon, several score of police marched up Des Plaines Street. Clubs at the ready, they pushed the crowd backward on top of itself, boxing us into the canyon made by the Crane Works like Indians before a massacre.

Bonfield's lackey, Captain Ward, shouted that he and his men planned to break up the meeting, peaceable though it was so far. Not wanting to succumb to the McCormick strikers' fate, I shouted back "Like hell!" and I threw the missile into the middle of the policemen's ranks.

After the bomb exploded, its concussion still reverberating through my chest, everybody froze, caught in the instant between an irreversible act and the panic which follows. Then the remaining policemen, whose trigger fingers already itched, picked themselves up off the pavement and opened fire on the crowd. Demonstrators ran pell-mell out of the smoke and filtered into the nearest alley or street. From the vestibule where I was shoved by the police and from where I threw the bomb, I escaped by running east along Randolph Street with some of my fellows. Behind us, bullets zinged through the air like so many angry bees, hornets and wasps. To give an idea of the ferocity of the battle, one journalist reported that a wall closest to the clash had nearly two hundred bullet holes chewing it apart.

When we were several blocks away, the sounds of a furious riot still reaching our ears, about twenty of us bid hasty farewells to one another, and we disappeared into whatever hiding places we could find. To their very great credit, none of the fellows with whom I escaped ever came forward to give the police my description.

SPUNGKDT. So that's why you weren't ever identified.

GHOST. That reason, and the fact that the police never took any notice of me like they had of the leading speech makers and writers whom they singled out for the hangman's noose.

STARK. You keep saying "leaders." I didn't think anarchists had any leaders.

GHOST. Yes, definitely. There was a very great number of factions in the anarchist movement, each with its own leader. Those who belonged to the Knights of Labor were considered by everyone in the labor movement to be the most forward thinking. Parsons and Spies were the most revolutionary of the Knights and the most eloquent.

SPUNGKDT. Card-carrying communists, huh?

GHOST. Pshaw! Spies and Parsons, those so-called anarchists, in truth possessed what I would call Socialist beliefs. I quit their bunch because they were such talkers—talking at picnics, talking at parades, talking in meeting halls, always talking, talking, talking. As if picnics and parades would succeed at overthrowing all the capitalists and industrialists, yellow-jacketed cowards who would have their mercenary armies shoot you dead if you dared raise your voice in favor of shorter hours or safer conditions.

STARK. Sounds like Spungkdt and me—neither one's a real joiner.

GHOST. After I quit the Knights, I joined the *Lehr-und-Wehr-Vereine*, a German-speaking club devoted to the pursuit of skill with firearms. Like me, my fellow members disgustedly threw down their picket signs and became men of action. In our meetings at the northwest edge of the city, I learned how to shoot pistols and rifles, and I was taught the techniques of manufacturing dynamite bombs. It was my favorite, a pipe bomb, which I threw at the phalanx of police.

SPUNGKDT. And you blew up something like ten cops.

GHOST. I wish it were more! I read the bomb killed a total of two. Eyewitnesses said that the police, those blithering idiots, dove into alleys and cowered under shop awnings shooting at their own men. This fact accounts for the rest.

STARK. So why did you do it?

GHOST. A multitude of reasons. But not for the reason that was proclaimed at the Haymarket Seven's trial by Mr. Grinnell, the prosecutor: that the inflammatory words which Spies, Parsons, &c., wrote or spoke incited me to throw the bomb.

Oh, it was true I saw a handbill they printed up announcing the meeting that contained the infamous line, "Workingmen arm yourselves and appear in full force." But, though I did see the handbill in question, working as I did in a printing house along Fifth Avenue, only a couple hundred were printed up, and Spies did not distribute them to the general population. Words or no words, I planned all along to bring my bomb, and I planned to throw it, too, if my fellow workers were threatened by the police.

It also was true that most, if not all, of the men on trial had spoken publicly of using force as a means to attain our ends. It appeared we would be forced to take up weapons against the capitalist classes, for peaceable means such as the ballot did not work. Witness how the city fathers stole the 1878 aldermanic election from Parsons, who ran on the Workingmen's Party ticket and won the most votes.

No, my reasons were not because of words, but rather because of deeds: the horrendous deeds robber barons like George

Pullman, Marshall Field, Cyrus McCormick and Philip Armour perpetrated against my family and my fellows.

When I was a child, a tremendous tide of anti-German Know Nothingism washed over the city. Worried over the increasing numbers of foreigners moving to the city, whom they accused of stealing work away from native-born Americans, these men had the city government fire all the foreign-born workers in the various departments at City Hall. My father, a man who spoke fluent English as well as German, and who was justly proud of his job as a city clerk, was one. He never recovered from the broken heart they caused him, and he died only a little while later, jobless and penniless, thereby leaving me to pursue a printing apprenticeship rather than affording me the chance to finish the higher grades and possibly attend the university.

And after the Great Fire of 1871, these men and their cronies pocketed millions of dollars in relief money the workers of other cities sent the workers of Chicago to help rebuild their homes and places of employment. A dozen years had past, yet the disgraceful living conditions suffered by the vast majority of the city's population had not improved one iota. About six months before the Haymarket Riot occurred, hundreds of starving men, women and children protested outside the Board of Trade building on the eve of its dedication. Safely locked inside, I'd wager that even with a near-riot happening beneath their windows, the men sitting on the Board of Thieves never tasted one ounce of nausea as they gorged themselves on duck and quail spooned up from their twenty-dollar-a-plate ceremonial dinners.

In short, it became quite clear to me that words were of little use when dealing with such greedy, cowardly men; only a bomb such as the one I threw at the Haymarket would send the message that we workingmen meant to improve our lots.

SPUNGKDT. So your impression is that the guys who were hanged were all words and no action?

GHOST. That is correct. No matter, since the trial was a fraud and a sham. No witness ever positively identified any of the men as the bomb thrower, and, although the police planted some bombs in Louis Lingg's living quarters before they searched them, he was never proven to be the bomb maker. Why, the sitting judge, Judge Gary, his mind made up in advance concerning the Seven's guilt, ignored the proceedings altogether. I read in the labor press that he spent the entire trial flirting with some young hussy sitting on his lap.

The trial came down to words, and words alone: did or did not the anarchists declare their intentions of overthrowing the existing order? But, with headlines like one I remember, which read "Damn All Anarchists To Hell," the verdict handed down by the court was a foregone conclusion.

SPUNGKDT. And all this happened in a country which prides itself on its Bill of Rights.

GHOST. Precisely.

STARK. You ever regret throwing the bomb?

GHOST. Never for throwing the bomb. That was a decision I made as an individual. Independent action for a just cause, even a violent action, is always a thing for which a man can pride himself. That's true anarchism.

However, a very tremendous guilt has lain over me for never turning myself in to the authorities. Even Albert Parson's heroic surrender to the court, when he came out of hiding to stand trial with his comrades, did little to sway my mind. Had I come forward, I possibly could have saved the accused from being condemned.

If I had been a braver man, I might have shared their notoriety, too; instead, I remained alive and well, but history forgot me, or rather history remembered me as an anonymous character. The men who were hanged for my action soon came to be called the "Haymarket Martyrs" and achieved worldwide fame because of the heroics they displayed in their last moments on earth. Standing on the gallows, George Engel went so far as to declare, "This is the happiest moment of my life." On account of that statement he shall be remembered and loved by all workingmen everywhere for as long as men care to remember the brave words and deeds of heroes like him. True, he never raised his hand against his foes, yet, perhaps after all, words are mightier weapons than dynamite bombs.

But, alas, I chose a different fate, a very dishonorable one by comparison. For the rest of my life I kept my secret to myself; I even withheld from my wife the fact of my crime. I already have related to you the pride I feel for my act, but I feel a great amount of shame as well, since I let four innocent men go to the gallows in my stead. Such a mixture of feeling is like eating a holiday meal every day—filling up to the point of discomfort by turkey, dressing and pie. Unfortunately, I never could loosen my belt enough to relieve my discomfort, nor could I ever fully digest my shame.

That, I suppose, is why I have returned one hundred years later, for I have the blood of innocent men on my hands as well as the blood of two policemen.

SPUNGKDT. Maybe you wanted to save yourself so you could throw another bomb sometime. Maybe you wanted to keep the Movement going and all that . . .

He didn't respond, however; instead, the ghost of the guy who threw the Haymarket bomb was enveloped in that weird blue flame again, followed by thick white smoke which dispersed after a minute or two. With that, Stark turned off his tape recorder, and we headed back to our loft, no longer hungry, which accounted for us being out in the first place, but feeling a queer mixture of panic and exhilaration.

And later, I couldn't sleep. The whole night long I had terrible nightmares peopled with goblins, demons and ghosts, only they were dressed in navy blue suits like bankers, lawyers and brokers.

# 17 Total Strangers: Part Three

As it turned out, Clay was drummer with The Strangers for little more than two months. He quit when he got an offer to work as a studio musician in Los Angeles. When I asked him about his move, he said, explaining the fringe benefits, "All the toot you can snoot, and all the chicks you can squish, Ish."

With no one else lined up to take the place of Clay, Rudy asked Stark if he would like to rejoin the band. Stark didn't have anything else going musically, so he agreed. During the subsequent eleven months the band improved markedly, and even played a handful of gigs at some local clubs. But I noticed two or three months into Stark's tenure a growing edginess in him, and found myself wondering how much longer he would stick with the band.

The night that Stark quit the band for good proceeded like any other night spent with the band. Going on were the usual things: the squabbling, the patching up of squabbles, the shuffling of new musicians, and the sporadic playing of music. On this rather historic night, a Sunday, I was lying on the couch, reading the *Sunday Tribune Magazine*, finding myself contentedly detached from the bitching, moaning, coaching and cajoling. Like top forty radio, which is full of too much talk between the same songs played over and over, the band filled the Sangamon Street airwaves, turned down and largely ignored, but nevertheless keeping me company.

After awhile, the band put down their instruments and gathered around the desk during their break. I tuned out their conversation and kept reading my magazine; the novelty of the band had long worn off for me, and I no longer felt impelled to stick my nose in their business.

"I'M SICK OF YOU SHITTING ME!" I heard Stark yell suddenly. This was followed by the sounds of him punching the hanging lamp above the desk, the lamp bouncing off the ceiling like a steel tetherball, and the pop of the bulb exploding. Glass flew in every direction, including some shards which landed on my chest between my chin and the magazine propped up on my stomach. I didn't want to get involved at all, so I acted like I still was reading, but my attention single-mindedly was fixed on the drama enacted behind my head. The last thing I heard during this excruciatingly intense interval was Stark marching into his room and slamming the door behind him.

When a few moments had passed, I sat up and looked around at the rest of the band's reaction. Everybody looked dumbfounded at first; then Rudy and Danny snapped out of their zombie stares and brushed flecks of glass off their shoulders and laps.

"Well, I guess that's it. I know somebody quitting the band when I see it," Rudy said finally. With the lamp still swinging overhead, everybody packed up his equipment and left. Wanda, the last person to exit through the big steel sliding door, blew me a kiss and waved good-bye.

With the street door downstairs safely shut, Stark came back out of his room. The smile on his face erupted into uproarious laughter. Joyfully beating his knees with his fists between paroxysms, he joined me in the living room. He examined the lamp, which no longer was swinging, but now slowly revolved. A round indention, where Stark had punched the lamp, spun by me, followed by a six-inch-long straight dent, created when the lamp rebounded off a skinny pipe mounted on the ceiling.

"That was *hilarious* the way you just kept reading as if nothing happened when I biffed the lamp," Stark said, his laughter showing no signs of subsiding.

"Well, hats off to *you* for quitting the band, and with such style," I responded, beginning to laugh myself.

"What did they do after I left the room?" he asked.

"Well, they looked pretty stupefied for a while. Then they picked up and left."

"I see they didn't take their P.A. or amps. That means they'll be back at least one more time."

"You could arrange to have them come on a week day," I suggested. "I'd be willing to stick around and let them in. That way you wouldn't have to deal with them."

"No good. Rudy's got a key, remember? He can come and go anytime. He'll probably slink in and out on his own, and we'll come home late and all their crap will be gone. Probably half our stuff will be gone, too."

"What made you go off like that?" I asked.

"You weren't listening?"

"Not at all. Lately, every time Rudy started talking, I tuned him out. My brain automatically switched to a different channel."

"If I could have done that, I might still be in the band," he said.

"So that's the official word? You've quit the band for good?"

"That's pretty clear, don't you think?"

"I guess you're right," I said. "Rudy took it that way. But then it always seemed like a misbehaving dog—you know, like you had to hit him across the face with a newspaper and yell 'No!' really loud before he listened to you."

"That's for sure. And then he'd accuse you of being uncool and an asshole if you did spout up."

"So you never answered my question. Why did you quit?" I asked.

"We should be out gigging once or twice a week. That's the only way to get any good. Look at Hank Damask. He was a pretty lame guitarist when we first met him, and then he went on the road with that reggae band, and now he's really come into his own. That came from playing three or four shows a week for two years. But instead of doing what we were supposed to be doing—playing straight through our set lists and choreographing a show—everybody was always arguing about who slept with who last week. I don't have to tell you that that shit gets real old real quick."

"I was amazed you stayed in the band so long. You don't have much patience with most other things."

"I kept believing if I stuck it out a little bit longer, something would happen. Rudy always tried to act all promising and reassuring. He'd say shit like, 'We record just one more demo tape and we're on our way.' But I see now that he was just diverting attention away from his lack of results."

This reason Stark gave for quitting the band was of course the main one, but lots of smaller reasons were mounting higher than the garbage piles on some of the vacant lots around the neighborhood. The following consists of all the trash I dug up on The Strangers, amounting to a number of articles, great and small, that I picked through to explain why Stark quit the band.

## *Rudy Tells One Too Many Whoppers*

Stark and I returned to the loft one Sunday night while Rudy the Roach and company were in the midst of band practice. We had just seen the movie *Sid and Nancy* at the closest theater to where we lived, the Chestnut Station, up around Clark Street and Chicago Avenue.

Pissed off and wanting relief from the teeny-bopper punk rockers sitting in front of us, who threw popcorn at each other during the whole movie, Stark persuaded me to walk home rather than catch a cab. Our walk through the Post-Industrial Urban Apocalypse was a silent, unpeopled, head-clearing time. But the composure Stark regained from walking disappeared the closer we got to our loft, especially after strains of Rudy's song "Super

Mental Masturbators" came into earshot when we were two blocks away.

I understood this reaction completely, for, in those days, Clay was still the band's drummer, and Rudy was dragging his feet in searching for other quarters. It looked as if The Strangers would rehearse at our place indefinitely, despite the obvious hints we dropped for them to clear out their stuff. One day Stark went so far as to tape onto Rudy's guitar case clippings from the real estate section of the newspaper which advertised spaces for rent to artists and musicians. A month later they still could be seen when Rudy carried in his guitar, but he never appeared to notice them, or, more in character, he simply chose to ignore them.

Nobody paid us any attention as we entered through the big steel door, then sat down in the living room area. With the band continuing to play, we had to shout to one another our comments about the movie.

"That sure was one dissipating flick," said Stark.

"Sid Vicious died from dissipation," I said.

"I think we ought to ask Rudy about Sid Vicious. What do you want to bet he'll say something like he and Sid used to shoot up together?"

Soon the band broke off playing, and Wanda, Rudy, Clay and Danny sat down with us. "What've you two urban cowboys been up to?" Rudy asked.

"Trying our best to avoid you guys," was what I hoped Stark would say, but instead he said, "Watching the Sid Vicious flick."

"I saw that," said Wanda.

"How was it?" asked Rudy.

"I thought it was a pretty authentic depiction of the dissipatory lifestyle," I said.

"Yeah, except for the sappy ending," said Stark. "After he kills Nancy and ODs in jail, there's this scene at the end when he walks out onto a pier, meets her in a taxicab, and they drive off into the sunset."

"I liked the ending," said Wanda. "I thought it was romantic."

"I think it seriously undercut the dissipation theme," said Stark.

"You don't think spending eternity with your mate is romantic?" asked Wanda. "It reminded me of the Dracula film, where they buried Frank Langella and his lover in the same coffin together. That scene practically made me wet."

"I thought you weren't supposed to tell the ends of movies," said Danny.

"Did you ever meet up with Sid Vicious?" I asked Rudy, then winked at Stark.

"No, I never met him."

Stark's eyes widened like he couldn't believe his ears. It seemed, for once, that we had come up with the name of someone from the counterculture whom Rudy didn't claim to know personally. But then Rudy amended his negative answer.

"Tell you what, though," he continued, "I used to live in the same room that he and Nancy lived in at the Chelsea Hotel. It was about six or eight months after he killed her there. They cleaned the blood up off the rug and everything, but you know what? There was a big splotch of dried blood on the wall inside the closet. I think she crawled in there and that's where she died. It was pretty absurd—they repainted the room and cleaned the rug, but they didn't bother to paint inside the closet."

"Oooh, that's creepy," said Wanda.

"I don't think I have to tell you what kind of bad vibes were in that room," said Rudy. "I had to move to another room after awhile."

Stark just shook his head. It was possible, logistically, for Rudy to have known all the people he said he did. But I could tell that Stark was drawing the line with this particular story. It was like listening to a priest trying to convince some doubting soul that the reliquary by the altar contained Joan of Arc's kneecap.

"Boy, Sid sure does sound like an asshole," said Danny.

"He's not anybody I'd want to party with," said Stark. "But he's okay fifty feet away on a movie screen."

After a momentary lull in conversation, Clay piped up. "Hey, Stark. Don't be a mope. Bring out your dope."

"We're out," I said.

"Damn," said Clay. "And I was looking forward to catching a good buzz and watching *Monty Python* when I got home."

Since no marijuana was forthcoming, which eliminated all reasons to stick around, everybody in the band packed up and left.

Upon hearing their cars drive away, Stark asked, "You know what?"

"What?"

"I'm beginning to think that I feel the same way about Rudy as I feel about Sid Vicious," he said.

"How's that?"

"That he'd be much easier to take fifty feet away on a movie screen."

## *Wanda Hits the Stage*

Things were looking up for The Strangers. Rudy the Roach had landed them a steady gig. I say "steady" as steady goes in the Chicago rock club scene, which meant for this particular string of dates every Monday night during the month of March. An hour before the first show I was lugging drums out of the back seat of a cab and into the front door of Stash's, a bar on the west edge of the Lincoln Park neighborhood. The drums were encased in bulky, round containers more difficult to maneuver than the plain drums themselves. After my second trip I decided to call it quits; I may have been a groupie to The Strangers, but I sure wasn't going to be any roadie. Besides, I didn't want to deal any further with the cabbie, who acted sullen the entire ride, probably because Stark and I sat with him in the front seat, while the drums rode in the back.

As I watched over Stark's equipment inside the door, a cigar-chomping, white-haired, fiftyish guy, who, despite his age and smoking habit, was wedged into his jeans like he worked out regularly, asked, "Why dincha use the back door?"

"Uh, I don't know. These aren't my drums," I said.

"The stage is in the back. Take that stuff back there. And watch my wood. Don't bash inta anything."

"Okay," I said, irritated at Stash, who was acting like an ex-cop. I picked up a side tom case, and, mindful of Stash's admonition, I tight-roped my way through the dark bar, juggling the big, but light, container while teetering between table and chair sets on my left and a thirty-foot long bar to my right. Three-quarters of the way back, I heard again, "Why dincha use the back door?" Stark had entered with more equipment.

As Stark proceeded to set up his kit, I surveyed the room. It appeared uniformly brown: the masonite walls were painted brown, the floor was brown linoleum, and the raised details stamped into the tin ceiling were obscured by layers of brown lacquer. Built of walnut, the bar was also brown. With nobody new to harass, Stash busied himself by buffing patches of the bar with a soft cloth. I had to admit he was justly proud of the gloss he achieved with his wood.

"I think this is a neighborhood bar trying to pass itself off as a rock club," I said, turning to Stark.

"I'll say," he said. "Check out this dinky stage. It must be three feet square."

Stark exaggerated downward, but not by much. The stage, built against the wall, was no more than six feet square, and had a waist-high railing surrounding two of its sides, with the back side open.

With his bass drum and pedal assembled, Stark pulled a hammer and several ten-penny nails out of his tool kit. He began to pound a nail into the stage floor flush with the rim of the bass drum.

"What the shit is this?" asked Stash, suddenly sticking his head over the railing.

"I'm anchoring the bass drum. It creeps forward when I play," said Stark.

"Pull that nail up outta that board. What's the matter with you?"

"I do it all the time at other places."

"Well, you ain't doin it here. Let me go downstairs and get some bricks. Watch the bar," he said, directing this command to me.

"Bricks don't work, asshole, and neither do cinder blocks," Stark said, once Stash had disappeared through the back door.

When Stash returned, he gave Stark a couple of bricks, which Stark reluctantly arranged against the bass drum. "Gonna hafta take a tube of plastic wood outta the night's receipts," he grumbled while retaking his place behind the bar.

A few minutes later Rick O'Shea arrived. Having given up on finding a lead guitarist, Rudy had invited Rick to play keyboards in the band. Rick had rewritten all the guitar solos for his instrument, oftentimes cutting them by half of their original lengths, an act I was grateful for.

"You know, there's a back door," said Stash.

"No, I didn't know," answered Rick, holding his synthesizer under his left arm. "Give me a pint of that rum," he said, pointing at the carryout liquor behind the bar and holding out some bills with his free hand. As Stash handed Rick his rum, I finally got up the nerve to ask this very cranky bartender for a beer.

"You with the band?" he asked, eyeing me with suspicion.

"No, not really. I'm with the band, but I don't play *in* the band."

"That'll be two bucks then. I always make it a policy to give the band free beers."

"That's nice for the band," I said, then turned to face Rudy, Wanda and Danny, who were fumbling with guitar cases, amplifiers, microphone stands, and coils of wire.

"What's happening, Stash?" asked Rudy.

"Nothing so far, except I gotta plug a hole that drummer of yours made in my floorboard."

"I hope you showed him the error of his ways," said Rudy.

"Damn straight I did. Listen, you start at nine-thirty. You hafta get off by midnight, or else the neighbors complain."

"No problema," said Rudy, then he, Wanda, Danny and I joined Rick and Stark. After opening his guitar case, Rudy pulled out a stack of dog-eared flyers and handed them to me. "Ish, take these up and leave them by the door."

Walking to the front of the bar, I read the flyer. A piece of promotional material that Rudy concocted, it contained a line which described Wanda as "tall, beautiful and riveting." I already had mentioned to Stark that when Wanda sang, her feet seemed like they were riveted to the floor; I couldn't resist laughing out loud at Rudy's ironic choice of words. The last line of the flyer sounded a bit overblown: "If you're tired of black clothes, black humor and black thoughts, then catch The Strangers, your antidote for a black disposition." Leave it to Rudy, I thought, to write a manifesto, when some sexy photos of Wanda would have had twenty times the impact.

To prevent Rudy from sending me on any more errands, I sat and drank my beer at a table mid-way between the door and the stage. Turning around, I observed a young, burly guy wearing a Stash's baseball jersey, maybe Stash, Jr., pull up a stool by the door to collect the money.

Nine-thirty came and went, but the only paying customers were a group of four young women, all of them dressed in black leather jackets and sporting short, angular haircuts, plus Stark's sister Suzanne with two of her friends from work. Unhappily, the latter group sat at my table.

I say "unhappily" because, after a brief romance, during which time I accompanied her to blues clubs, Mexican restaurants and hot tub spas, Suzanne and I had recently stopped seeing each other. Given our recent history, I was terribly uneasy about the seating arrangements.

"We're going to the bathroom. Watch our purses?" she asked.

"Sure," I said, then gulped down my beer. In their absence I reminisced about the romantic nighttime walks Suzanne and I took along the train tracks that passed close by the loft, a place I had named the Sangamon Scenic Overlook, where we discussed our fantasies, stopped to make love in the weeds, and gazed together at the skyline, our own private Milky Way, from the best vantage point in all of Chicago.

When Suzanne and her friends returned, she said that her friend to my right, Theresa, brought along some cocaine, and she asked if I wanted some. I declined and saw my opportunity to escape. "I'm going to see what the hold-up is," I said, excusing myself. In addition to the discomfort of sitting next to an ex-girlfriend, I didn't relish the idea of being a purse-watcher all night during their dozens of trips to the bathroom to snort their coke.

"It's early yet," Rudy said, explaining why the show hadn't begun.

"We wait too much longer, and we'll have to cut the second set short," said Rick, plinking at the keys of his synthesizer.

"Not to mention it's Monday night," continued Rudy. "People need time to recover from the first day of the work week before going out."

"I meant to ask you about that," said Danny. "Mondays are deadsville. Why did you get us these gigs on Monday night?"

"The way I look at it, it doesn't matter if nobody shows the first night. Word still gets around. Next week there'll be more people, and then the following week even more. It takes a while for the snowball to get rolling."

"From what I remember from my snowman-building days, you have to have a core to roll the snow around," said Stark. "We don't have a core group here."

"Like I said, it doesn't matter. Look at the Ramones," said Rudy.

Anticipating still another round of name-dropping, Stark, Rick and I rolled our eyes in unison.

"I remember talking to Joey Ramone once," Rudy began. "He was telling me about the early days at CBGB's. He called it nothing but a 'shit bar' and said the only audience they had for their first few gigs was the bartender's dog. A few weeks later he said the Warhol crowd started showing up, and then the band took off. I think he was saying that it can happen anywhere, in any bar. It could happen here. We could be discovered tonight, in this very bar." While Rudy was droning on about Joey Ramone, his eyes grew bigger and bigger, like they were filling up with helium. I thought they just might float out of his head and off into the realm where dreams are stockpiled.

"If nothing else, we have a chance to play all the way through our set list," said Rick.

"Yeah, for once," said Stark.

Suzanne and her friends excused themselves as they walked through our group on their way to the bathroom. I was off the hook; they carried their purses along.

"Say, Ish," said Rudy, pulling me off to the side, "I noticed that Suzanne and her girlfriends are visiting the head pretty often, even for women. Are they doing coke tonight, or what?"

"Well, they said they had a little bit, but I don't know if they're willing to share," I said.

"It's not for me that I'm asking, it's for Wanda. As you probably noticed, she's a little down in the dumps." He pointed at Wanda, who sat on a chair with her head between her knees. "I know that you and Suzanne are going out. I thought since you're on the inside track, you could maybe talk them into turning Wanda on with a little, you know, to help her wake up."

"To tell the truth, I broke up with Suzanne. You talk to her."

"I'll do that," he said, then walked over by the ladies' room and hovered around the door, waiting for Suzanne to emerge. So *that* was why Wanda always acted so moody, I thought: far from being a reformed coke freak, like Rudy claimed the first night I met him, she probably did it all the time, and whenever I saw her, she was either high as a satellite or hurtling back to earth.

"Hey, how about starting the show," one of the women in black shouted.

Upon completion of Wanda's trip to the bathroom, she bounded onto the stage to join the rest of the band, and they kicked into the first song of the night, "Downtown," which had become a sort of theme song for them. "Remember!" Stash yelled at them over the opening chords, "Be off by midnight."

Wanda certainly cut a striking figure fronting the band, or, to be more precise, she stuck out well from the rest of the group crowded together on the tiny stage. The clothes she wore, a white tee shirt ringed by a blue necklace, a leather miniskirt, black fishnet stockings, and high heels, were clean for a change. She was more alert than I think I ever saw her, and she appeared to have shaken all the clumsiness out of her joints. Best of all, she belted out Rudy's lyrics like a pro, no doubt due to ingesting the cocaine, which sparked her nerve endings to a degree of high voltage. Her enthusiasm, however artificially induced, was contagious. I was madly tapping my foot on the bar's footrest.

Wanda's stage presence infected the band, too—Danny and Rudy playfully crashed their shoulders together while they strummed their guitars, and Rick bobbed his head to the beat between sips from his rum bottle, which he set on top of the keyboard above his left hand. Even Stark looked pleased; I caught him breaking into a smile on several occasions. Although another two or three patrons came through the door and settled into the audience, I hoped nobody in the band noticed the disappointing turnout, for a glance by any one of them out into an empty bar could've transformed their confident, aggressive performance into a shaky, self-conscious mess.

As if to confirm my worries, serious troubles arose after just four songs. Wanda's pitch started wavering, and her tempo began to drag noticeably. Immediately I hit upon the reason why: the fifteen-minute cocaine buzz had worn off, thus leaving her to her own devices to complete the set. I half-expected Rudy to interrupt the performance and send her back to the bathroom where she could refuel herself.

Wanda continued her deceleration. After the song "Pepsi Cola in Petrograd" she dopily unfastened the microphone; then, like a fireman sliding down a fire pole, she hooked her arms around the mike stand and slid down it. Only she didn't hit the floor running like a fireman, she just hit the floor.

The next song, "Bludgeoning Love," described a couple so powerfully in love they couldn't control their emotions enough to stop beating each other up. Thematically speaking, Wanda's kneeling on the stage worked; she gave the impression that the female party in the relationship was beaten into submission. However, when the band started the next song, "Super Mental Masturbators," a snappy, up-tempo tune, she failed to rise again to her feet. For the rest of the night she stayed there on the floor, alternately crouched on all fours or sitting sideways on her hip, which caused her skirt to hike up and reveal her black lace panties. When she didn't muff the words to Rudy's songs, she mumbled them into the microphone. On some verses she sat out altogether, prompting Rick to play the melody line on his synthesizer.

"Wake her up!" one of the women in black hollered. Indeed, there was some effort on the stage to do just that. Rudy kept shouting down at Wanda while the band played, and in between songs, Stark thumped his bass drum repeatedly, trying to get her attention back. With each beat of his drum, she shook her head from the shock, but she never pulled herself up off the floor. Too bad they didn't have roadies, I thought—one could have come onto the stage and stood her up on her feet.

At the end of the set, to the sounds of sporadic clapping and taunting howls, Wanda leaped up and raced off the stage into the back of the bar. This feat must have taken all her remaining energy to accomplish. Rudy handed his guitar to Danny and followed her into the ladies' room; even given the distance to the bathroom from where I sat, I could hear all kinds of yelling, crying and fist pounding from behind the door. After a ten-minute interlude with Wanda, Rudy walked out of the bathroom alone and approached the bar. I was all-ears.

"You know how it is with bands," Rudy said to Stash. "They have good nights and bad nights."

"It's the same with bar owners," said Stash. "I don't think I hafta tell ya this was a bad night for me."

"I promise we'll be better next week. I'll make sure Wanda gets her beauty sleep."

"Well, I'm afraid there ain't gonna be no next week. You guys didn't bring in enough customers to make it worth my while. I didn't even make enough money tonight to pay my doorman. Granted he's my son, but I still gotta pay him. I'm willin to break even with bands comin in here, but when I come up short at the register, I just gotta say no cigar next time. Sorry."

"But you agreed we'd play here every Monday night for a month. You aren't going back on your word, are you?"

"We ain't got no contract. It was just a handshake deal, and handshakes don't mean nothin. This is a tough town. Everyone shakes your hand with one hand and knifes you in the back with the other. I'm sorry, Rudy. But I gotta make a livin. That's the same answer you'd get from anybody in my position."

"It's been a real slice, Stash," said Rudy, turning and walking back to help pick up the stage.

"When you got a guaranteed audience give me a call," Stash called out to Rudy. "Then we'll talk about a second chance."

Standing behind the stage waiting for Stark, I listened to everyone's gripes concerning the night's proceedings.

"This was one lousy night," said Rick, zipping the vinyl cover over his keyboard. "I don't mind buying my own bottle of rum, but I draw the line when I don't make enough money to pay for it."

"Was she on the rag or something?" asked Danny, rubbing the neck of his bass guitar with a cloth.

"Sometimes I really hate this town," said Rudy, peeling up wires duct-taped to the floor. "Full of working-class stiffs who'd rather go bowling than see a band."

"You ever get the idea that this band is like an airplane ready to take off, but all it does is taxi down the runway and never lifts off the ground?" asked Stark, unscrewing his side tom from his bass drum and placing it back in its case.

## *Rudy Hires Then Fires Rick O'Shea*

One Saturday afternoon in July, Stark and I were sitting on the sidewalk across the street from the loft in a spot we had designated the "Sangamon Beach." Behind the beach was the "Sangamon Prairie," a vacant lot now by mid-summer overgrown with the biggest thistles I had ever seen, huge stalks with broad spiny leaves. In front of us was the curb, where scraps of paper and styrofoam cups washed over the gutter like whitecaps. We sat shirtless, our chests glowing red from a good dose of sun; Stark sat on a folding chair, and I sat on a drum, not a real drum from his kit, but a souvenir Indian drum Stark got as a kid from the Wisconsin Dells. The radio was tuned to the public station, which was airing "Mambo Express," their regular Saturday afternoon show.

"It doesn't get any better than this," I said, quoting a beer commercial we had seen on TV.

"Yeah. Who needs to live in a yuppie high rise with a pool on the roof, when we have our very own private beach," said Stark.

"I don't know," I said. "The water might be nice to jump into. We don't have that."

"Yuppies don't go swimming, either. They just sit on the deck flexing their health club muscles and spilling their drinks. That's pretty much what we're doing, only we're not paying the steeped-up rent."

"Well, if you squint your eyes a certain way, I suppose the street looks sort of like a river."

"Face it. The street's an undiscovered tributary to the Sangamon River."

"Whatever you say."

A little while later, the first car we had seen in an hour appeared. Our eyes always followed any car that passed when we sat out front of Sangamon, if only to assert territorial impulses to passers by. Suddenly, this car, a squarish brown one, screeched to a halt, and the driver shifted gears, throwing it in reverse straight towards us. I for one was snapped out of my reverie, but not so alarmed yet that I felt like diving into a thistle bed behind us. Still, at moments like this, the mind sees all kinds of terrifying things; I flashed on gang bangers opening up on Stark and me with machine gun pistols.

It was Rick O'Shea who leaned across the front seat and said out the passenger window, "I see you guys are home after all. I wasn't even paying attention to this side of the street, really, I was casing your windows to see if anybody was home. Then I see these two crazy-ass guys *sun-tanning* in the rear-view mirror."

"Pull up a seat on the Sangamon Beach," said Stark.

"That's not your regular car," I said to Rick.

"My car's in the shop," said Rick. "This is a renter." Then he peeled out, cascading us with dust and gravel, and made a U-turn to park on the other side of street. As he crossed the street to join us, he pulled off his shirt.

"Got some lotion upstairs," said Stark.

"I can't believe this scene. You're surrounded by all these factories catching some rays," said Rick, obviously impressed, and Rick, a crazy-ass himself, was not easily impressed.

"On the weekends we *own* the neighborhood," Stark responded. "We're giving new meaning to the term 'meat market.'"

"It's time," I said, when the disk jockey broke into the music and announced it was three o'clock. At my cue, Stark and I stood up, realigned our chairs, and sat facing the Sangamon Prairie with our backs to the sun. "Don't want to fry our fronts," I explained to Rick, who sat down cross-legged on the sidewalk facing us.

"So that was Rudy's decision, huh?" asked Stark.

"Yep. I'm fired from the band," said Rick.

"Rudy put it like you were laid off, not fired," said Stark. "Either way, it was a typical near-sighted move."

"He told me he 'clawed a hot guitarist' and that keyboards 'don't fly in this town,'" said Rick.

"Did you tell him that keyboards don't fly, fingers do?" asked Stark.

"There wasn't any talking him out of it, it was a done deal," said Rick. "From what I gather, there were rehearsals I wasn't told about, and you guys had been practicing with this guitarist behind my back for a couple of weeks."

"We've had other singers sit in, too, behind Wanda's back. It's a recurring subplot with the band," said Stark. "I would've said something if I could, but Rudy made me promise not to tell."

"I'm not pissed at you. It was Rudy who connived it all," said Rick.

"Knowing Rudy, he'll probably ask you back in a month," said Stark. "That's the average life span of lead guitarists in the band."

"The real kicker is that we had some paying gigs lined up," said Rick. "I could've used the extra money."

"I think we have two gigs in the next six weeks. That's windfall money, not extra money," said Stark.

"But it turned out fine," continued Rick. "Jeff Bresniak—remember him? the drummer from the reggae band Hank and I played for?—he got me a marching band gig at Great America."

Stark and I busted out in laughter.

"Seriously. I've been playing tenor sax in a marching band the last week and a half. A true nine-to-five job."

Stark and I couldn't stop laughing.

"It's a complete hundred-piece marching band, with drum majors and color guard and everything. We march through this huge amusement park playing Sousa tunes, a half-hour on, a half-hour off. When we're off, Jeff and me ditch our uniforms and duck into 'Park Personnel Only' places to smoke a joint. Let me tell you, with Jeff playing stoned jazz in the drum line and me playing blue notes on the sax, we've got the whole band playing Bourbon Street Sousa by the end of the day."

"I don't think I could handle all those people when I was stoned," said Stark.

"It's a *blast*," said Rick. "There's everything to feed your senses on: people, cotton candy, hot dogs, Looney Toons characters, ferris wheels, merry-go-rounds, balloons, kids, roller coasters, popcorn, pretzels, puppet shows, more weird people, *everything*. I can't believe I'm getting paid for it."

"What do you say we run some time trials?" I said, after a short lull in conversation spent by the three of us concentrating on the heartbeat-skipping timbale parts coming from the radio. In the most animated state I had seen all day, Stark folded up his chair, gathered up the radio, and led Rick and me upstairs so we could put on the appropriate clothing for time trials.

Rick, a bit bewildered by all of our frenzied activity, soon caught on when we returned downstairs and rolled my motor scooter out of the lobby and into the street. It was with my scooter that Stark and I tested our nerve by racing it around the block while the other timed the trip with a stopwatch left over from Stark's more athletic teenage days. Although my scooter contained a tiny two-stroke engine that prevented you from going more than a tame thirty miles per hour, with all the sharp turns and other assorted obstacles there remained the wipe-out danger, which accounted for us changing into jeans and putting on shirts.

"I'd put your shirt back on if I were you," said Stark to Rick. "Or else it could be Hamburger Helper time."

Rick complied, and I fired up the scooter. To warm the engine I rode up and down the block a few times, then pulled up to Stark and Rick, who together marked the starting line.

"Ready . . . Set . . . Go!" said Stark, and off I went on the course we had mapped out.

The first challenge the rider encountered was the intersection of Lake and Sangamon, a four-way stop. You lost time if you slowed for the stop sign, so I beeped the horn and gritted my teeth in a prayer for anyone coming down Lake Street to obey the sign and stop, because I wasn't planning to. At Randolph Street you hung a left inside the boulevard separating where trucks parked in front of the produce stands and the street itself. Doing this you avoided the stoplight and a busier cross street than Lake. However, there were still hazards: you had to slalom between any cars backing in or out, and you possibly could face the grill of a truck coming straight your way.

At Green Street, two blocks east of Sangamon, you hung another left and rode the wrong way up a one-way street. Once the turn was made, you immediately had to lean left to dodge a nasty pothole we had earlier identified, a maneuver which forced you to take a tight left turn down Wayman Street. On Wayman your vertebrae could fly off your spinal cord like beads if you sped up too much, due to the uneven brick pavement, cement patches covering the brick, and asphalt patches covering the cement. At Sangamon you turned left one final time and accelerated till you passed the finish line, indicated by the lamppost out front of our building.

"Two-oh-two point seven," said Stark, when I pulled back up to him and Rick. "Not very good."

"I was taking it easy for my first ride," I explained.

"No guts, no glory," he responded.

"You go," I said, then handed the scooter over to Stark. When he nodded that he was ready, I said, "On your mark . . . get set . . . Go!" and I punched the stem of the stopwatch with my thumb. He took off, leaning on the horn from the very start and huddling down as he shot through the stop sign at Lake Street.

"Stark always needles me on my time," I said to Rick. "Even when I have a good time, he manages to shave a second or two off. He's unbeatable."

"He didn't make the same turn you did," said Rick, looking into the distance.

Sure enough, Stark blew through the stoplight at Randolph and continued south down Sangamon.

"Looks like he's deviating from the course," I said. Convinced it would take Stark a while to return, I explained to Rick the proper course to take in anticipation of his upcoming ride, focusing especially on hazards like the stop sign, the pot hole, and the bumpy brick street.

When I completed my explanation, I glanced down at the stopwatch. "He's been gone over seven minutes," I said.

"Maybe he stopped for a mid-afternoon snack," suggested Rick.

At that moment, Stark buzzed through the nearby four-way stop, only he was traveling east down Lake Street.

"Looks like he's lost all sense of direction," said Rick.

"It looks to me like he's joy-riding instead of running a time trial," I said.

A minute or two later, after making the original course's final turn from Wayman to Sangamon, Stark reappeared and casually rolled to a stop.

"Eight-thirteen point seven," I said. "By far the worst time ever recorded."

"Where did you go?" asked Rick.

"I was bored with the course, so I rode down to the Grid to see if there were any alternate routes. You know, to spice things up a little instead of going around and around in circles."

When mentioning the Grid, Stark meant the very grim thirty-six square blocks bounded by Randolph to the north, Halsted to the east, the Eisenhower Expressway to the south, and Ashland

Avenue to the west. The area was perfectly bisected by Madison Street and the attendant Skid Row scene, which provided the only signs of life within the boundaries of the Grid, although what few people appeared there seemed to us more dead than alive. The rest of the Grid was a ghost town even during week days; all that could be seen were block after block of dilapidated warehouses, the rubble of buildings long-ago burned down, vacant lots overtaken by weeds and refuse piles, enough boarded-up storefronts to start a failed business merchant association, dozens of abandoned automobiles, and the occasional rabid dog.

"I made an interesting discovery about the Grid," said Stark. "It's like a coloring book."

"How's that?" I asked.

"Because it's in color when you're there. It's in black and white when you're not there, but it's in color when you're there."

"That's pretty profound," I said, somewhat sharply, still irritated he took so long for his time trial.

"Time for your turn," said Stark, dismounting, then pointing at the seat for Rick to take his place.

"Are you ready for this?" I asked, worrying about turning my scooter over to a neophyte.

"I've ridden a few bikes in my day," said Rick. "In high school we used to ride dirt bikes."

"Well, this scooter here doesn't go near as fast as a dirt bike would," said Stark.

"The principle's the same, though," I said. "Dirt bike trails are probably smoother than certain sections of the Sangamon Race Course."

"What's the record time?" asked Rick.

"I did it in a minute thirty-six once," said Stark.

"I'll keep that in mind," said Rick as he climbed onto the scooter.

At Stark's signal Rick tore away from us; when he hit the four-way stop, he didn't even beep the horn, he just shot through the intersection going full speed.

"Did you see that?" I asked. "He didn't even hesitate at the stop sign."

"I think he's out to beat my record," said Stark. "But then he always was a reckless dude."

This was a true fact, no better exemplified than when he climbed things. You see, Rick had a habit of climbing anything and everything tall. He climbed up simple things like fire escapes and trees, of course, but he also climbed more difficult things as well, like smoke stacks, water towers, utility poles, and cliffs along the Mississippi River (or so we heard). Once, when the three of us were trekking through the Post-Industrial Urban Apocalypse, Stark and I dared him to climb a rickety old gantry crane that straddled the train tracks. Not only did he climb up to the walkway at the top, a feat neither Stark nor I ever attempted, he stayed up there while a commuter train roared by underneath. Evidently, he had the itch to climb things since his childhood; he told us that once, while vacationing in New England with his family, he angered his dad by climbing up to the crow's nest of the Mayflower replica in Plymouth and hollering "Ahoy!" in every direction. From what we had seen so far of his time trial, Rick had an affinity for speed as well as heights.

"Here he comes," I said, pointing up the street.

"He's taking the turn a little wide," said Stark.

"Uh oh. I think he's going to hit the curb. If he doesn't wipe out first."

Rick's perilous situation out of our hands, Stark and I braced ourselves for the worst. We watched as Rick, no longer able to keep his balance, and my scooter's tires, no longer able to grip the pavement, be overwhelmed by centrifugal force. Barely across the finish line, Rick flew off the bike head-first and nearly smashed his face into the curb; the scooter fell on its side and skidded down the street until it ran out of momentum and stopped. Stark ran over to see if Rick was hurt, and I hurried over to cut the scooter's engine.

Fortunately, although he had some scrapes and bruises on his forearms, Rick appeared not to be seriously injured. Understandably, he rose to his feet a little slowly; however, though he was shaken, he was more concerned about his time than any potential broken bones.

"It's amazing I had the presence of mind in all this excitement to stop the stopwatch, but I did," said Stark. "One twenty-eight point one—eight seconds under the record."

"Way to burst the envelope," I said, congratulating Rick on his record, one that was never broken the entire time we conducted time trials.

"That's one way of dealing with getting kicked out of the band," added Stark. "Go the self-destructive route."

## *Wanda Takes Off Her Shirt*

The night Wanda took off her shirt was hot. But not the definition of hot that describes clapping and hollering men gaping at a showgirl taking it off. Rather, it was Chicago-in-mid-August hot; it felt like all the chemicals polluting the air were adsorpting into a thick paste that covered every inch of your skin. To make matters worse, the neighborhood around Sangamon stank like a thousand refrigerators were thrown open, each one emitting powerful smells of spoiled meat, sour milk and rotting cantaloupe.

Adding to the close environment was the band, over for its usual Sunday afternoon practice. The loft had the air of a gymnasium too crowded for people adequately to exercise. I say this because they still had not played a song all the way through, even after two hours. They'd play through a couple of verses, but when they got to the chorus, everybody would stop and drink a can of beer. That is, all of them except for Wanda, who drank peach-flavored New York Seltzer. It was during one of these breaks that Wanda took off her shirt.

"They say it's the humidity, not the heat," said Danny, their bass player.

Although I thought this observation was self-evident to anyone who lived in the Middle West, I didn't have the energy to shift everyone to a different topic of conversation.

"When I lived out west," I said, "it got to ninety or a hundred degrees, but it was fine, because the humidity was like eight or ten percent. It was semi-arid country."

"I wish some of that semi-arid shit would blow in here," said Stark.

"I wish I were out at Coney Island right now," said Rudy, "with a cooler full of margaritas in mayonnaise jars."

I tried to imagine Rudy on a beach, wearing the clothes he was then wearing, his usual outfit, consisting of a charcoal gray, long-sleeved work shirt, black jeans, and black steel-toed work shoes. The way his clothes hung so loosely off him, I would say that if he ever went ocean-side and took off his shirt, he would be the runtiest guy on the beach. Now, none of the rest of us guys had especially great physiques, but at least we were dressed for the weather with our shirts off. Stark and I wore only gym shorts and shoes, and Danny wore flowered Bermudas.

Wanda was wearing a turquoise leotard, with a billowy, cotton-print skirt tied around her waist. She had long since tossed off her pumps; as she ran around barefoot, I found myself worrying that, given her klutziness, she might walk through a glassy patch of floor and cut up her feet.

Regarding Rudy's dress, she must have been thinking along the same lines as me, for she suddenly said, "Why don't you take your shirt off, Rudy? I don't think I've ever seen your chest except when we have sex." She winked at Stark and me. Stark looked nauseated by her joke.

Rudy demurred. In response, Wanda said, "We'll both take off our shirts."

Then she did it: she pulled down the straps to her leotard, uncovered her breasts, and arranged the leotard around her waist like a belt.

"Put your shirt back on, Wanda," Rudy said. "You're embarrassing the other guys." This was true; all of us turned away, and suddenly the mood became very uncomfortable. Stark looked mortified.

"Why? We're all adults here. It sure beats roasting in our skins. C'mon, honey, take your shirt off, too."

Rudy acquiesced, and, break over, everyone except me returned to the band area, all of us averting our eyes from Wanda's chest.

Since Wanda's back faced the rest of the band, everyone gradually became less distracted—despite their shaky start on "Pepsi Cola in Petrograd," they eventually settled into the proper groove. I normally sat behind the desk, out of eyeshot from the band, but with Wanda bare-breasted, I sat at the kitchen table, a place which afforded an unobstructed view, and pretended to read a magazine.

Without being too obvious, I periodically snuck glances at Wanda. In between singing verses she nonchalantly fanned herself with an *Elle* magazine, as if nothing was out of the ordinary. To this day I believe that she meant nothing prurient by taking off her shirt; indeed, she appeared innocent of the fact that her breasts had an impact on anyone in the room. Maybe in her modeling days she spent time dressing in front of photographers, lighting people and makeup artists, who, being professionals, were oblivious to her nudity. I got the impression that, like a naturist, she took off her clothes and figured that if people were offended, that was their problem. My naturist analogy broke down, however, when I noticed that she didn't have a lick of tan on her—except for her black hair, red lips, and maroon nipples, she was perfectly white, like the color of limestone.

Then it happened again: while gazing at her, for a fraction of a Platonic second I saw the feminine ideal, like Wanda had metamorphosed into a marble sculpture from ancient Greece, and all of her flaws fell away. With the blink of an eye, she returned once again to her normal self.

I'm not exactly sure how to explain it, but I have this capacity to see the essence of a woman, but only in short glimpses. When I was dating Stark's sister, I saw her in this fashion one morning while she reclined on the bed talking to me after I had spent the night. Maybe the sheets tangling around her like a toga affected my mind as if by some Hellenistic spell.

I often wonder if this phenomenon is supernatural. Or perhaps my friend Stevo's girlfriend suggested a better theory; though she never had set foot on Sangamon, she was pretty correct in pronouncing it a "male bastion." This implies a likelier explanation: I was starved for female companionship.

In any event, Stark didn't share my Hellenistic attitude; he appeared to adopt a decidedly Hebraic attitude toward Wanda. With a marked look of distaste, he announced that he was "having a heat stroke." He stood up, whispered a couple of words to Rudy, then took his fan into his room, presumably to lie down. Denied the services of their drummer, the rest of the band packed up, Wanda pulled her leotard up, and everybody left.

When the band had been gone for several minutes, Stark came back out of his room with his fan.

"Do you believe that shit she pulled tonight? I mean, that was totally crude of her," he said.

"She didn't mean anything by it, Stark," I said. "That's just the way she is. You have to love her for it."

"After tonight, I'm not sure if I even like her."

"You're such a prude."

"Look, I like women as much as anybody. But they have to know me pretty damn well before they can show me their chest."

## *A Walk Through the Post-Industrial Urban Apocalypse*

It was October, the time of year when trees turn yellow, red, purple and brown. That is, elsewhere in the Middle West far outside the city limits in suburban forest preserves, or up in the north woods of Wisconsin and Minnesota, places Stark and I dreamt of visiting. Left of the Loop we had no such trees to admire, only bushy, scrubby weeds growing in vacant lots or tall, grassy weeds zigzagging down cracks in streets. What plant life that grew there was leafy and green one day, then barren branches the next. If I didn't have a calendar telling me otherwise, I would have thought that fall lasted just one day.

Although shut off from fall colors in wooded landscapes outside the city, we nonetheless could enjoy the crisp autumn air by strolling through the Post-Industrial Urban Apocalypse, the only wilderness readily available to Stark and me.

"Check it out—total stillness in the middle of the city," said Stark, as he surveyed the half-mile-wide corridor stretching east from Fulton Market Cold Storage on Morgan Street all the way to the Chicago River, a ten-block-long expanse. "What do you call this place again?" he asked.

"The Post-Industrial Urban Apocalypse."

"Wait a minute," said Stark. "I thought where we're standing now was the Sangamon Track."

"It's the Sangamon Track when you jog. At night it's the Sangamon Scenic Overlook, because it's a good place to bring a date and impress her with the skyline."

"Have to be a pretty brave woman," said Stark. "Or somebody foolish brave like Wanda . . ."

"But when you take a walk and dwell on stuff, it's the Post-Industrial Urban Apocalypse," I said, finishing my explanation.

"A multi-purpose recreational area, huh?"

"You could call it that."

The consummate picnickers, I carried a frisbee to toss around later, and Stark carried along his boom box. Having had his fill of silence, he clicked it on.

"What's the name of this tape?" I asked.

"'Pardon My Torso.' It's one of my various tapes."

Stark was referring to one of many compilation tapes he spent whole Saturdays assembling. He would buy a hundred dollars' worth of records downtown, pick out the two or three best songs on each, record these songs on a various tape, then sell the records at a used record store up on the North Side. Choosing from a wide variety of music, Stark documented on these various tapes his passing enthusiasms with any number of guitar bands of the moment, like the Replacements or R.E.M., his respect for a handful of all-time rock and roll hits, and his taste in certain pop songstresses, like Dionne Warwick and Petula Clark.

Two songs into our walk the chromatic guitars of "Day Tripper" filled the air. "I'm into this Beatles stuff circa 1966," said Stark.

"They were a great garage band before they were the Beatles," I said.

On the heels of my Beatles pronouncement, we saw ahead of us what looked like a jogger. Sure enough, a clean-cut young guy wearing a Harvard sweatshirt, shiny blue designer running shorts, and spotless, expensive-looking leather running shoes, was approaching. When he was close enough to make out faces, we scowled at him as if to imply he was on our turf only by our good graces. As he passed, Stark said, rather tauntingly, "Hey, you lost? Lincoln Park's twenty blocks north of here."

The jogger chose to ignore this quip of Stark's. We followed him with our eyes till he turned north up Morgan Street, after which he vanished behind an abutment.

"Where do you think he came from?" I asked.

"He's probably some yuppie MBA that lives at the Haymarket Lofts."

"There goes the neighborhood," I said.

"If you ask me, we ought to strap a railroad tie on the front bumper of my van and ram all the BMWs that are cropping up around here," suggested Stark.

"Let's walk down the tracks," I said, because we had reached the point where concrete pavement ended and mud commenced.

"Good idea. I don't feel like slogging through this mess," said Stark.

Our change of direction brought us near a familiar stopping point: a two-block-long freight house, whose docks had long ago fallen into disuse. Pieces of worm-eaten siding, once comprising its exterior, lay half-buried in surrounding muck, and it was fenced off with Danger signs abounding. On a previous trip through the Post-Industrial Urban Apocalypse, Stark had tried talking me into scaling the fence and inspecting its interior. I told him all that was holding the structure up was soggy tarpaper, and the only way I would try that was "if I had a fresh tetanus shot in my ass."

Continuing again along the tracks, I noticed that the ties were overgrown with moss like fallen trees in the woods; this moss, along with rotting wood, emitted a sweet smell mingled with a sharp creosote smell. While watching where I stepped, I made a mental inventory of the objects strewn between the rails: uncoiled copper wire, chips of styrofoam packing material, an empty plastic bottle of motor oil, wads of newspaper, several six-pack rings, scruffy tangles of twigs, an indeterminate number of crumpled paper cups, a flattened paint can with dried blue paint squirting out both ends, a broken bottle of Mad Dog, twists of rusty steel, two flashlight batteries with sulfur oozing from under their caps, and filthy plastic sheets billowing like fallen ship sails.

"Whoa!" I said, stopping suddenly. Seeing I was spooked by something, Stark came to a halt and studied with me the object of my discomfiture: the spinal column of some small vertebrate.

"What do you think it's from?" asked Stark. "A dog, maybe?"

"Maybe a pig," I said.

"Let's hope it's not the remains of some little kid butchered by a pervert murderer," said Stark.

"I think we better go on the assumption it's a pig or dog," I said. The image of this spinal column sufficiently burned into our memories, we continued with our walk, this time veering left and wading through waist-high weeds toward an old spindly crane that teetered over a set of crooked train tracks. In a move traditional to every trip past this crane, I climbed the ladder up its side; like always, when I reached mid-way to the top, where a couple of rungs were broken out, I called it quits and climbed back down. Then Stark took his turn.

Stepping off the bottom rung, he said, "There's got to be a way to reach the undercarriage." He referred to the car which rolled underneath the superstructure of the crane. Planks of wood had fallen away from the sides of this car so you could see skinny gaps of daylight through it.

"The floor would bottom out," I responded.

We proceeded east down Kinzie Street, now a meandering gravel path with weeds on either bank. Just eight blocks west of the Chicago Loop, Kinzie Street resembled a picturesque country road, seemingly a million miles away from Kinzie Street across the river, where limousines dropped off jock executives at the exclusive East Bank Club, or rich men escorted their fur-accoutered wives into the jazz clubs and highbrow restaurants behind the Merchandise Mart.

"Here comes another small businessman," said Stark, observing a homeless man doddering among the weeds. Obviously dissipated, he paused every few feet and proceeded to pick all the twigs off arbitrarily chosen branches. He seemed to focus all his concentration on this activity and took no notice of us.

"I don't know why these homeless guys get such a bad rap," I said. "Pruning weeds is a useful contribution to society."

"Yeah, one not everybody recognizes," said Stark. "It says something about keeping one's own garden in order."

After walking under the Halsted Street overpass, the edges of a thirty-foot-tall dirt mound spilled into our path. For all practical purposes Kinzie Street ended, at least for the time being. Stark took off running up the slope; when he reached the summit, he raised his fists in a king of the hill gesture. I saw this defiant attitude in shadow on a retaining wall to his back, indeed a very striking sight.

"You should give it a try," he said, running back down. "Walter Payton trains on a hill like this. Only it's steeper."

"Well, he plays for the Bears, and I don't," I said, opting to pass on this particular amusement.

A few blocks further, underneath the Des Plaines Street underpass, Stark picked up a couple of bottles and tossed them at the piers holding up the bridge. Then commenced a mad scramble between the two of us for the substantial number of pint liquor bottles scattered on the ground, which we whipped at the cement, breaking them in rapid succession. Judging from the fire ring nearby, it was clear that some "small businessmen" recently had themselves an all-day office party.

We decided to head south toward Fulton Street. As we passed a big pile of broken cinder blocks, I pointed and said, "That's where I puked last spring when I walked home from bar hopping on Rush Street."

"You told me about that. Wasn't it like four in the morning?"

"Pretty absurd, huh? I can't say puking spoiled my good time, though," I said.

Just then a rat poked its head out of the rubble. Adrenaline throbbed through my trunk. Stark must have experienced a similar shock, for he stepped backward and said, "Lucky you didn't catch rabies that night."

"You're right. In the dark I couldn't see I was puking on a rat honeycomb."

Upon turning the corner onto Fulton Street, we ran across a fenced-in parking lot with about two dozen commuter buses parked inside; these buses were the ones which clogged the main arteries downtown by pulling up in front of luxury hotels and letting off businessmen who rode in from O'Hare Airport. It was a little curious, I remember thinking, that buses serving such a hoity-toity function were parked in such crappy circumstances: rusty sheets of corrugated siding leaned on the fence at various points, punctuating the flow of yellowed newspapers blown against the chain link and glued there by rain.

Outside the Fulton House, a high rise condominium complete with a marina on the adjacent river, a building located inexplicably in the midst of the Post-Industrial Urban Apocalypse, we decided we had come close enough to civilization and turned about. At that moment we crossed paths with a Buick containing two adults in the front seat and a grandmother and two kids in the back. For kicks we glared menacingly through the windshield to see if we could elicit any reaction from this ultra-normal family unit. Sure enough, we heard the doors' automatic locks click. As you can imagine, this caused untold amounts of guffawing on Stark's and my part as we walked away.

Upon returning to Halsted Street, we took a short detour off Fulton and headed onto the overpass, which arched above the Post-Industrial Urban Apocalypse. In the middle, at its highest point, we were afforded a decent aerial view of the surrounding landscape. To our left we saw a fleet of eleven refrigerator trucks parked outside the Ball Park Franks factory, each with "HYGRADE'S Meats" emblazoned in yellow across their navy blue sides.

"I wish I had a hot dog right now," said Stark, his taste buds triggered by these trucks.

"It's Sunday," I said. "Everywhere's closed."

"Let's jimmy the lock to one of the trucks. We could build a fire and have us a wiener roast."

Turning around after Stark's fanciful suggestion, we beheld the skyline. "Look, it's One Phallocentric Plaza, where I work," I said, turning Stark's attention to the fifth or sixth tallest building in Chicago. "Wouldn't it be great if we had a rocket launcher? If I aimed half way up, I'd probably take out a couple of floors of Sickly & Caustic."

"Everybody's off-work today. There wouldn't be any casualties," said Stark.

"You'd be surprised," I corrected. "Lawyers work eighty-hour weeks. At least a dozen potential casualties are up there right now, wasting their weekends. We'd be doing them a favor."

"I wish Rudy the Roach showed that kind of dedication." Stark's ongoing complaints with the band made their inevitable appearance, which was only natural given that, through taking a walk, we were attempting to scrub out the crud accumulated in our brainpans.

"You know what?" he continued. "I think we've stumbled onto the difference between Rudy and us. We think it's okay to jack around so long as you get the job done. With Rudy, as long as he smokes a little reefer, he considers it a good night, even if we sound like we've been banging pots with spoons all night."

"Do I detect a belief that Rudy the Roach is cynical?" I asked.

"He's beyond cynical. He's jaded," said Stark. "There's no flies on his songs, that's true. But I'm getting sick of the sideshow atmosphere. It wouldn't surprise me at all if one of these days he brings a rat geek by to sit in on lead guitar."

This sudden realization of Stark's explained a lot. It was now clear how seriously The Strangers were thwarting Stark's ambitions. For, even though he was the first to put his lips to joints when they were passed around, I saw the large amount of self-discipline he otherwise demonstrated for the band's benefit. After all, the reason we lived left of the Loop in the first place was to have rehearsal space for whatever musical projects came his way. Witness also his saving money for a year and a half to pay cash for a van, which enabled him to transport the band's equipment to gigs. With this painful truth uncovered, it would only take another month before Stark would send Rudy the Roach and what Stark called his "slack-jawed retinue" on their merry way.

# 18 Ice Age on Sangamon Street

Late in my tenure left of the Loop I traveled to Toronto with Fiona, a woman I met at my job, then fell for. Toronto is like a newer and cleaner Chicago; we found no evidence of any place left of the Loopish. During the short time we visited that city, we went to the rather touristy lake front area, to Casa Loma, a gigantic castle built by a rich industrialist at the turn of the century, and to the Royal Ontario Museum.

While at the Museum we strolled through all the rooms. We liked especially one particular room that contained dozens of antique musical instruments—early violins, straightened-out trumpets, serpents, lutes and, my personal favorite, an ophiclede, a cross between a tuba and a bassoon. Fiona and were experiencing newfound love; it was hard to say where the glints around the room came from—from the polished and restored instruments or from our eyes. Anyway, I wanted to see dinosaur bones next, so we headed to the natural history wing. I saw my dinosaurs, some a lot smaller than I expected, which disappointed me, and several with bones broken out of their tremendous rib cages, reminding me of pianos missing keys.

Exiting the natural history rooms, we saw a display which pictured a cross-section of the dirt deposits that various glaciers left behind when they spread out over North America. "Look," I said, "in between the Wisconsin and Illinoian there's a Sangamonium."

"Sangamon*ian*," Fiona said, correcting me.

"Stark and I must be living in the Sangamonian Ice Age," I said.

"Especially Stark," she said. "His brain is definitely in the ice age."

"You never mind," I said as we proceeded to the next exhibit on our list of must-sees: armless, headless Roman copies of Golden Age Greek statuary.

When we returned home, I decided to investigate the geologic activity during the Sangamonian era, which, so far as I could glean, carved out much of the region's geography. Maybe the rivers, creeks and streams presently funneling down the Mississippi River Valley—the waters that we drink containing the minerals that invigorate us—were the remains of Sangamonian glaciers melting away ten thousand years ago. The Great Lakes themselves might be vestiges of Sangamonian Pandemonium.

Turns out that there was no Sangamon glacier after all, but a time span between two glaciers known as the "Sangamon Interglacial Epoch." Geologists reckon that in the late Pleistocene Age, or about twenty to one hundred thousand years ago, a series of glaciers, like continent-wide rolling pins, came down from Canada, then rolled back up again. Based on dirt, rock and clay deposits they have found at various depths in the ground, geologists have identified four distinct glacial epochs, the Nebraskan, Kansan, Illinoian and Wisconsin, which were interspersed by three interglacial periods. Sangamon was the last of these.

The glacier immediately prior to the Sangamon Interglacial Epoch, the Illinoian, spread itself out so wide that it displaced the Mississippi River, shouldering it over into what is now Iowa. During its heavy rest, the Illinoian Glacier created what geologists call "Sangamon soil." According to one geologist, "[t]he stratigraphic name *Sangamon* derives from a widespread soil recognized and named in Illinois as early as 1873." Sangamon soil is characterized by how it has weathered and festered into a substance called "gumbotil," a dark, sticky, gumbo-like clay.

It's so sticky because calcium carbonate leeches out, and various silicate materials disintegrate; additionally, iron is slowly sucked out of the soil by vegetation growing on the surface four to six feet above.

Here was a scientific phenomenon familiar to a resident of Sangamon Street: dissipation in the form of electrons evaporating from the very ground we stood on. Yet there remained a troubling inconsistency: according to the books I was reading, interglacial epochs fostered a moderate, even mild, climate, whereas Stark and I suffered harsh weather conditions.

The most crucial meteorological factor left of the Loop was not, as some people hearing the phrase "Windy City" would think; although it was difficult to distinguish the roaring sound of elevated trains from winter gusts, the true determining factor was the skyline, a veritable mountain chain blocking our near west side abode from mild air resting over Lake Michigan. Comparing the skyline to mountains is not that far-fetched; practically every day I paused to gaze out the windows at the Sears Tower, located nine or ten blocks southeast of our loft, and felt a similar sensation while gazing at the Rockies a couple of years before while I was in grad school: the mountains were so massive that, miles away, they appeared to be right in front of me, only a stone's throw away.

Out west, coastal mountain ranges blocked the mild Pacific air from the land-locked college town where I lived, thus creating desert conditions. The sun, perched in a cloudless sky, baked and cracked the earth in summer; in winter the howling cold demanded exceptional measures to keep the limbs of inhabitants from freezing off.

Comparable weather patterns occurred left of the Loop due to the skyline: hot, humid air settled over us in July and August, hastening the decomposition of animal remains that filled dumpsters on every street corner. At the other extreme was bitter cold; one of the most vivid memories I have of living in our loft consists of Stark and me watching a Bears' playoff game in January huddled under blankets with our respective space heaters blasting lukewarm air at our feet. Two phrases Chicagoans always hear during weather reports are "cooler by the lake" in summer and "warmer by the lake" in winter; you can bet that Chicagoans living between the skyline and the lake didn't suffer our distress, for both meteorological and socioeconomic reasons.

Only later was I able to reconcile the disparity of Ice Age climatology and the chill factor we experienced in our loft. The resolution did not come about until new winds blew into our lives, casting Stark and me away from Sangamon Street. What I realize now is this: living left of the Loop was a time of *thaw*, an interval between the frozen ideas of school and what has come to be known as "the big chill," a point in life when all of us young rowdies supposedly grow up and become responsible adults, with spouses, kids and mortgages.

One afternoon when I was ill, a phone call to my employer, Sickly & Caustic, prompted me to quit my job. All day long I dreaded making this call, because my boss Layla had a knack for intimidating her workers into not calling in sick, on account of the interrogation she subjected them to over the phone. It wasn't enough if you were sick; you had to listen to her verbal abuse, too, thus making you feel doubly bad. Our conversation went something like the following:

"What do you mean, you're sick?" Layla asked.

"I'm sick."

"Are you hung over? Because if you are, you're not getting any sick time from me, no sir . . ."

"I think I have the flu or a virus or something."

"You don't know what you got?"

"The *symptoms*, Layla. The symptoms are like the flu—headache, body aches, chills . . ."

"You been to the doctor's? What does he say you got?"

"No, I haven't been to a doctor."

"Then how do you know you're sick?"

"Look, Layla, I'm sick. I'm not coming into work tonight."

"You thrown up yet?"

"No."

"You can't be very sick if you haven't thrown up yet. I need you here if you can make it. The department's swamped today; I been told there's two closings tonight, and now I'll have to pay somebody overtime because of you. You know those attorneys—they don't know nothing but work, work, work."

"I'm sorry." I tried to sound as pathetic as possible, which wasn't very hard since I was truly sick. "I'll try to come into work tomorrow."

"Well, I hope so. Call back if you feel better before tonight's shift. And if you aren't going to be in tomorrow night, you be sure to give me a call, y'hear?"

Fed up at last with all the abuse and disrespect dished out by Sickly & Caustic, I let Layla have it: "I QUIT! AND MAY YOU DIE DRIVING HOME TO THE SUBURBS TONIGHT IN A FIERY CRASH WITH A GAS TRUCK!"

Upon slamming down the receiver, I felt more exhilaration than most days when I wasn't sick; however, this emotion quickly turned to panic when I began to consider my prospects: money drawn on my last check from Sickly & Caustic would carry me no longer than three weeks, and I had no other job lined up. Also fueling my panic was the possible negative impact on future employment from quitting without giving the traditional two weeks' notice.

These concerns were laid to rest by the end of the week, though, when, in the midst of phoning law firms around the city to beg for a job, I talked to the document center supervisor at Beerbohlm & Klatsch. She had a very great need for proofreaders, because the firm was undergoing a conversion from one word processing program to another. Every document floating around the office needed proofing word-for-word to make sure no important language was lost in the process. Showing just how much she needed somebody with my skills, she offered me six thousand dollars more per year than I was making at Sickly & Caustic. I couldn't believe my luck: quit on Tuesday, start work someplace else I didn't expect the following Monday, *plus* a hefty raise.

My new boss, whom I found out later grew up in Springfield, Illinois, treated me well—I can vouch from experience that those of us who came of age in Sangamon country are decent, salt of the earth types. She even promoted me a short time later to computer operator, the same job Stark held for several years, although I had no previous experience with computers. What I appreciated most was crossing paths with somebody willing to give me a break, because she thought she recognized potential. At the helm of a two-million-dollar computer system, I started to regain the self-respect blistered away by daily lashings from that cat o'nine tails tongue of Layla.

A related development: my new job has allowed me to make peace with my conscience, for, compared to the contemptible clients Sickly & Caustic represented, Beerbohlm & Klatsch practices a more humane type of law. Revenue from a nationwide pizza parlor franchise and a chain of video stores accounts for a healthy chunk of my paycheck; no longer do I profit from toxic waste disposal or IUDs that rip up women's insides.

I have since shacked up with Fiona. We live in an apartment four blocks straight south of Wrigley Field, a much more hospitable environment than the West Loop to be sure—we have heat, hot water, and a roof not shot full of holes. We also have a color TV, a VCR, a piano, a computer and a microwave of our very own. Best of all, the floors are carpeted. But before the reader starts to think that the hero of this story is yupped-up, let me respond by saying that I still don't make the hundred-thousand dollar salary of a yuppie, nor do I go to restaurants because they're hip—I go because they're good places to eat. Give me beer and burritos any day; keep your wine and tapas.

A couple of months after quitting Rudy's band, Stark hooked up with Jake, his old guitarist friend from college who tutored him through his first year of rock drumming, and who now played in a heavy metal band called Alloy. Jake needed a drummer to go on his band's upcoming national tour, so he offered Stark the job. Mulling over his circumstances and determining that "I've pretty much spent my twenties in a marijuana cloud," he accepted. After just a few weeks of rehearsal, Stark's dream finally came true: he was on the road with a rock band full of motivated, business-like musicians. In the course of his touring, Stark has traveled around the continental U.S. three times, played dates in Canada, and flown overseas for shows in England, Germany, Sweden and Australia. So far, Alloy has achieved a fair amount of success, but only enough to pay Stark a modest living wage. Yet, with every album they record, the group's popularity grows, and I think that in a short time Stark will become a rock star. Even now, you can follow his career and look at pictures of him in certain trade magazines.

Best of all for Stark's mental health, he moved out of our loft on Sangamon Street, leaving the place vacant to this very day. He now lives in one of Chicago's northern-most suburbs where the band makes its headquarters.

By contrast, I fear my behavior resembles that of a middle class square these days, like I'm a six-foot cube of ice slurrying from home to train to work. This trend concerns me most in relation to poetry; absent the trials and tribulations living left of the Loop, my poetic faculties have all but lost their charge, like car batteries that die in sub-zero weather. Aside from taking an occasional vacation with Fiona or observing raving mad lunatics shouting obscenities on the Howard Street L, my life at present lacks adventure, and no thaw permeates things like when I lived on Sangamon. Therein lies the difference between Stark and myself: unlike me, Stark considers his present life a welcome thaw compared to his years on Sangamon, where he lived in a state of frozen animation.

I don't see much of Stark these days, but whenever he returns to town in between tours, we get together. One of our favorite places to meet is on the Sangamon Track, the quietest, most head-clearing spot either of us has encountered up till now. The neighborhood more or less looks the same, although there are signs of change. For example, the building next to ours has been torn down to make way for a paved, fenced-in parking lot reserved for employees of the new commercial photo lab around the corner. Also, rumors have been circulating that the Bears organization wants to build the team a new stadium on the near west side. When I saw a map of the plans in the newspaper, I noticed that the site of our loft was within the gray boundaries of a gigantic parking lot. Political squabbles amongst the city, team and community groups probably will prevent the stadium from ever being built, but no matter, for I've heard another story of a truly visionary plan for Sangamon: a real estate baron is thinking of leveling the area and building a gambling/shopping center/amusement park complex, a place that promises to be both Las Vegas and Disneyland of the Midwest.

Before that occurs, however, I have determined to freeze my own vision of the West Loop during the years I lived there by penning this story. Between feeding data tapes into computers, chunks of time when there was nothing to occupy me but listen to the computer room's sterile hum, I scribbled down as much of the experience as I could remember. It probably is just as well that I'm no longer writing poetry, because despite its reputation for heightened seeing, deep feeling, sensitivity to language, blah blah blah, a poem could never paint all the corners left of the Loop, a subject too big for any poem to do it justice. Indeed, after filling up forty-seven legal pads, I concluded that I had a book on my hands, and the guy who wrote that book had to have eyes, ears, throat and heart big as a forty-eight hundred square foot loft on Sangamon Street.